DATE			
AUG 12 '86			
DEC 14 1987			
AUG 25 1995			

The Constitution and the Budget

A Conference Sponsored by the
American Enterprise Institute for Public Policy Research

The Constitution and the Budget

Are Constitutional Limits on Tax, Spending, and Budget Powers Desirable at the Federal Level?

Edited by
W. S. Moore and Rudolph G. Penner

American Enterprise Institute for Public Policy Research
Washington and London

Library of Congress Cataloging in Publication Data

Main entry under title:
The Constitution and the budget.

(AEI symposia ; 80B)
Proceedings of a conference sponsored by the American Enterprise Institute for Public Policy Research and held in the spring of 1979.
Includes bibliographical references.
1. Budget—United States—Congresses. 2. Taxation—United States—Congresses. 3. United States—Constitutional history—Congresses. I. Moore, W. S. II. Penner, Rudolph Gerhard, 1936–   . III. American Enterprise Institute for Public Policy Research. IV. Title. V. Series: American Enterprise Institute for Public Policy Research. AEI symposia ; 80B.
HJ2052.C646   353.0072'2   80–23735
ISBN 0–8447–2179–4
ISBN 0–8447–2180–8 (pbk.)

AEI Symposia 80B

Printed in the United States of America

Contributors

Paul M. Bator
Professor of Law, Harvard Law School

Charles L. Black, Jr.
Sterling Professor of Law, Yale Law School

James M. Buchanan
University Distinguished Professor and General Director of the
Center for Study of Public Choice, Virginia Polytechnic Institute and
State University, and Adjunct Scholar, American Enterprise Institute

Arthur F. Burns
Distinguished Scholar in Residence, American Enterprise Institute,
and Distinguished Professorial Lecturer, Georgetown University

James Dale Davidson
Chairman, National Taxpayers Union

Anthony Downs
Senior Fellow, The Brookings Institution

Robert P. Griffin
Senior Fellow, American Enterprise Institute

Gerald Gunther
William Nelson Cromwell Professor of Law
Stanford Law School

Richard G. Lugar
United States Senator (Republican, Indiana)

Bruce K. MacLaury
President, The Brookings Institution

James T. McIntyre, Jr.
Director, Office of Management and Budget

W. S. Moore
Director, Legal Policy Studies
American Enterprise Institute

Contents

PART THREE
CONSTITUTIONAL RESTRICTIONS ON THE POWER OF THE PURSE AND THE THEORY OF PUBLIC CHOICE

PART FOUR
A ROUNDUP OF THE POLICY ISSUES RAISED BY PROPOSALS FOR CONSTITUTIONAL LIMITS

Foreword

AEI's Conference on the Constitution and the Budget, held in May 1979, generated the papers, commentary, and discussions that make up this timely volume. If anything, the pressures for balancing the federal budget, dampening inflation, increasing defense spending, maintaining and increasing social welfare spending, and combating recession have intensified since our conference took place. The only pressure that has not increased is the demand by the states for a constitutional solution to the problem of federal fiscal restraint. The number of states petitioning the Congress for a convention to amend the Constitution has remained constant at thirty.

As our publication date approaches, the pressures for a tax cut are growing. President Carter's ephemerally balanced budget for the 1982 fiscal year, based in large part on a tax increase, crumbled as the unexpectedly deep recession and other surprises reduced revenues and increased expenditures. The kind of tax cut necessary to improve the economy's health is being addressed in the 1980 election campaign. Our experience since the conference confirms that the problem of what to do about the federal budget is growing more acute.

A balanced federal budget was once the rule in the United States, not the exception. Since 1960, the budget has been in deficit every year except one. At the same time, the ideal or goal of budget balance or budget surplus has been modified by the notion that the budget should be in deficit in a time of recession and in surplus during prosperity. The past twenty years, however, have seen deficits during both good times and bad.

Our failure to exercise budgetary discipline, a period of unprecedented peacetime inflation, a growing tax burden, and the success of California's Proposition 13 have focused attention on public sector fiscal discipline. This volume addresses the dilemma of how to improve federal fiscal discipline without impairing the flexibility of Congress to respond effectively to national security needs as well as to the economic and human needs of the people.

Fiscal restraint may involve tax or spending limitations as well as constraints on borrowing or deficits. But as this volume reminds us, budget balance may not prevent rapid increases in tax burdens and spending. This book examines constitutional limits on budget making: would they improve legislative actions, or would they lead to less effective policy making because of rigidities imposed by constitutional amendments and the practical difficulty of enforcing them? Among those who favor constitutional limits, a subsidiary debate occurred between those favoring a ceiling on total spending and those who would require only a balanced budget. The book also examines the fascinating perplexities of a constitutional convention if thirty-four states call for one. While the issues addressed do not yield to definitive answers, our contributors shed considerable light on the problems, the difficulties associated with most of the proposals for reform, and the factors that must be considered in any attempt to make federal fiscal policy work better in the future.

WILLIAM J. BAROODY, JR.
President
American Enterprise Institute

Preface

John Maynard Keynes believed that "ideas of economists and political philosophers, both when they are right and when they are wrong, are more powerful than is commonly understood. Indeed, the world is ruled by little else. Practical men, who believe themselves to be exempt from any intellectual influences, are usually the slaves of some defunct economist."[1] The vigorous movement at the local, state, and federal levels to limit tax burdens, spending, and/or budget deficits may be an exception to the Keynesian rule. This movement seems to have been truly inspired by "practical men" working at the "grass-roots" level.

While state constitutional limits on operating deficits and specific tax burdens have a long history, it was the passage of California's Proposition 13 that caught the attention of the national media and federal politicians. The intellectual community was, generally speaking, caught by surprise and noticed for the first time that steadily growing numbers of states had quietly passed resolutions calling for a federal constitutional convention which would amend the Constitution to require a balanced federal budget. After Proposition 13, the movement could no longer remain quiet. Subsequently, the march toward a constitutional convention seems to have slowed somewhat, but by the spring of 1979, the call for a convention had passed in thirty of the thirty-four states necessary to bring such a convention into being.[2]

Apparently, many backers of the state movement do not actually desire a constitutional convention. Instead, they hope to prod the United States Congress into initiating a budget-limiting amendment of its own. Numerous resolutions have indeed emerged and are now being considered in hearings. The sheer number of variations on the theme is impressive. The most common resolution would simply prohibit deficits that are not sanctified by some qualified majority, say, three-fifths or two-thirds. Others would limit spending, most often as a share of GNP,

---

[1] *The General Theory of Employment, Interest and Money* (New York: Harcourt, Brace & Co., 1965), p. 383.

[2] There is debate over the legitimacy of some of the resolutions. See the discussion in part one of this volume.

and still others would both limit tax burdens and require a balanced budget.

Because of this outpouring of political activity, the American Enterprise Institute decided it would be useful to hold a conference in the spring of 1979 to explore the great variety of issues raised by the various initiatives to amend the Constitution. The goals of the conference were modest. We believed it more important to identify all the important questions than to answer a few questions definitively. To aid us in this task, we invited panels consisting of current and past public officials and scholars in fields relevant to the issues. Their prepared statements follow, together with an edited transcript of the informal discussion between the panelists and the audience.

August 2, 1979   W. S. Moore
                                                         R. G. Penner

Part One

Amending the Constitution by Convention

Introduction

W. S. Moore, Chairman

The last time this country held a federal constitutional convention was in 1787. As we approach the two-hundredth anniversary of that remarkable gathering, we are also approaching, for only the second or third time since 1787, the serious possibility of another constitutional convention.

By some counts, as many as thirty of the required thirty-four states have petitioned Congress to call a constitutional convention to deal with the problem of federal deficits. The possibility of a convention raises a number of unanswered questions: Does Article V, the amending article, contemplate only the kind of convention that occurred in 1787, that is, one to write a basic charter of government? Or does the article permit convening a convention to deal with a specific area of concern, such as federal spending and deficits, or the manner of election of senators, or apportionment of state legislatures?

Perhaps Article V permits either kind of convention and other possibilities as well. On the other hand, maybe Article V authorizes only one kind of constitutional convention. If so, what is that particular kind?

The states have the power to refuse to ratify the proposals put forth by a convention, and it takes only thirteen states to nullify the work of any convention—or the work of Congress, for that matter, when it proposes constitutional amendments. In addition to the ratification power of the states, what outside checks and balances exist to restrain a convention? What is the role of Congress, of the states, and of the federal courts?

How do states go about applying for a convention? What constitutes a valid petition? How should convention delegates be chosen? How would a convention be funded? How long would it deliberate?

In 1971 and again in 1973, Senator Sam Ervin's bill to spell out procedures for calling a convention passed the Senate. Had this measure been enacted, it would have answered some of these questions, but it would not have answered the fundamental question, which is the extent of Congress's constitutional power to legislate on the subject of a constitutional convention. Few areas of constitutional law are as unsettled and fascinating as this one.

Constitutional Roulette:
The Dimensions of the Risk

Gerald Gunther

Our remarkably brief Constitution has had only twenty-six amendments in its history. All have been adopted using only one of the two amendment methods provided by Article V of the Constitution: they were proposals adopted by a two-thirds vote of Congress. The present balanced budget campaign seeks to use the second method, relying on the Article V provision that "on the Application of the Legislatures of two thirds of the several States," Congress shall "call a Convention for proposing Amendments."

The fact that we have never used the convention method does not make it illegitimate, of course: it is there in the Constitution, and it is there to be used when appropriate. But it is an uncertain route because it has not been tried, and because it raises questions that have not even begun to be resolved.

If thirty-four state legislatures deliberately and thoughtfully decide to take this uncertain course, fully aware that they risk calling a convention that will be able to consider issues ranging well beyond the budget, so be it. But in fact, the ongoing campaign has been largely an exercise in constitutional irresponsibility—constitutional roulette or brinksmanship, one might say—a stumbling toward a constitutional convention that more resembles blindman's buff than serious attention to deliberate revision of our basic law.

The campaign has won the support of thirty states, but almost all these showed remarkable inattention to what they were really doing. The legislative debates by and large were brief and perfunctory—essentially up-and-down votes on whether one was for or against balancing the budget. Yet what was adopted, typically, was a resolution saying that, unless Congress submitted a budget amendment of its own, the state was applying under Article V for a convention. The questions of what such a convention might do, and especially whether it could and would be limited to the budget issue, were largely ignored.

A major reason why so many serious questions have been ignored is that the advocates of the budget amendment have given assurances that the convention will not get out of hand. In my view, there is no adequate basis for those assurances, and certainly not for the confidence with which they were presented. I believe that the convention route promises uncertainty, controversy, and divisiveness at every turn. With respect to the central constitutional question—whether a convention could and would be limited to a single object—I am convinced that there is a serious risk that it would not.

One way of beginning an examination of the problems is to scrutinize the assurances of the budget amendment advocates. There are three recurrent themes. First, we are told that a convention is not likely to come about, since the real aim of the drive is to spur Congress into proposing a budget amendment of its own. That claim seems to me the simplest to challenge. If the movement is to be a threat to induce congressional action, it needs to be a credible threat. A strategy that rests on the threat of a convention must surely take into account the possibility that a convention will actually convene.

Second, we are assured that any convention would be limited to the subject matter of the state applications. That is of course the central constitutional problem, and it raises a number of questions for which there are no authoritative answers. Let us concentrate for the moment on what Congress could and would do, and especially what a convention could and would do, if thirty-four valid state applications are adopted and Congress does not propose an amendment of its own.

Congress would probably heed the concern that stirred the applications and call a convention with a scope broad enough to still the qualms about excessive limitations. Congress might, for example, call a convention limited to the issue of fiscal responsibility—one that could consider the spending amendment supported by Milton Friedman as well as the balanced budget proposal supported by Governor Brown. And, if Congress took that route, it would presumably enact (at last) some legislation concerning machinery for a convention, something similar to that proposed by Senator Ervin a decade ago and recently reintroduced by Senator Jesse Helms. This sort of legislation presents a troublesome set of problems of its own, problems well worth exploring.

But such a congressional call would open the door for a new set of uncertainties and difficulties. Even if Congress were satisfied that the quite specific budget applications constituted valid "applications" and that it had the power to confine a convention to a particular subject (both debatable assumptions), that would not resolve the problem of what would happen at the convention itself. The convention delegates would gather after popular elections—elections where the platforms and debates would be outside congressional control, where interest groups would seek to raise issues other than the budget, and where some successful candidates would no doubt respond to those pressures. Those

6

convention delegates could claim to be legitimate representatives of the people. And they could make a plausible—and I believe correct—argument that a convention is entitled to set its own agenda: they could claim that the limitation in the congressional "call" was to be taken as a moral exhortation, but not as a binding restriction on the convention's discussions. Under that view, the subject specified in the call would create no more than a presumption as to what a convention should consider, a presumption that could be overcome if the delegates clearly perceived in their election campaigns wider areas of interest among the voters. And thus, the convention might well propose a number of amendments—amendments speaking not only to fiscal responsibility but also to such issues as nuclear power or abortion or defense spending or mandatory health insurance or school prayers. Under that view, a relatively narrow convention is possible, but certainly not guaranteed.

Now, if the convention were to report to Congress proposals going beyond the fiscal issue for submission to ratification, the argument would of course be made that the convention had gone beyond the proper bounds. Some claim that Congress could easily invalidate the efforts of any such "runaway" convention by simply "ignoring" the allegedly unauthorized proposals. But I believe that a congressional veto effort would run into substantial constitutional counterarguments and equally substantial political restraints. Consider the possible context—the legal and political dynamics—in which a veto of the convention's proposals would be considered. The convention delegates could make powerful arguments that Congress's refusal to submit their proposals to ratification would thwart the opportunity of the people to be heard through the ratification process. In the face of arguments such as those, might not Congress find it impolitic to refuse to submit the proposals?

That brings us to the third reassurance about the low-risk nature of the convention route. We are told that the requirement that three-fourths of the states must ratify a proposed amendment guarantees that the convention will not run amok. But there is a fatal flaw in that argument as well. There is a large part of the spectrum between narrow proposals and "run amok" ones. Can we really be confident that there are no issues of constitutional dimension other than a balanced budget that could conceivably elicit support in three-fourths of the states?

True, it can be argued that there is no reason to worry if there *is* ultimate support for ratification. But I am concerned about the *process*— a process in which serious focus on a broad range of constitutional amendments does not emerge until quite late. Is it really deliberate, conscientious constitution making to add major amendments through a process that begins with a mix of narrow, single-issue focus, inattention, and ignorance, that does not expand to a broader focus until the

7

campaigns for electing delegates are under way, and that does not mushroom into broad constitutional revision until the convention and ratification stages?

My understanding of the convention route can be attacked as making the process terribly difficult to use: the argument goes that state requests for a convention will be severely inhibited if single-issue applications can mushroom into multi-issue convention proposals. My understanding can also be attacked as construing the state-initiated amendment route as different from (as well as more difficult than) the traditionally used amendment process where Congress initiates. It can be attacked, moreover, for not trying hard enough to find a "mediating" position that assures a sensible reading of Article V consistent with modern needs.

I think those criticisms are vulnerable for many reasons, reasons I hope we will explore. For now, let me simply note that the criticisms overlook important historical lessons. True, the 1787 convention—which was itself a "runaway" convention, of course—deliberately gave the states the opportunity to initiate the amendment process. It is not true, however, that it made the state-initiated route nearly identical with the congressionally initiated one. The records of the 1787 convention are quite illuminating on this. As just one important event, the convention did *not* accept a proposal by James Madison to make two-thirds of the states coequal with Congress in proposing amendments. Instead, it limited the states' initiative to one of *applying* for a convention, and it inserted the *convention* as the institution that would undertake the actual proposing. That convention step inevitably makes the state-initiated route a different alternative, not a synonymous or even closely parallel one.

I would note, too, that the notion of a convention most familiar to the framers in 1787 was precisely the kind they were attending in Philadelphia—one that undertook a major overhaul of an unsatisfactory basic document. I do not mean to suggest that any convention called under Article V must be as far-reaching as that one. But I do believe that the convention contemplated was one that would consider all major constitutional issues of concern to the country. True, if the budget were the only major issue before us today, a single-issue budget convention might be entirely feasible. But the unavoidable problem today is that there *are* other constitutional issues of concern; and, if they are of concern, the convention may, in my view, consider them.

A convention capable of considering a broad range of issues—this is what the preponderance of the historical evidence as well as the constitutional text suggest. It is nevertheless argued that one may reinterpret an important structural provision in light of modern needs. Even

8

granting that assumption, I do not perceive a compelling case that there exists such a contemporary necessity. My view does not deprive the states' initial concern with a particular issue of all force, but it does emphasize that a convention is serious business, as I think it was intended to be and as I think it should be. Moreover, the case for viewing Congress as the major body for initiating amendments is reinforced by a structural consideration. Congress is ordinarily our one national deliberative body. Thirty-four state legislatures acting individually are not likely to take the initiating task as seriously, and thirty-four states operating separately certainly cannot engage in the kind of discussion possible in the national forum on Capitol Hill. Our recent experience with the budget campaign illustrates this point forcefully.

But even if my reading of Article V is unacceptable, we cannot deny that the convention route presents many questions, many uncertainties, and no authoritative answers. Surely, then, it ought not to be taken without the most serious thought about the risks ahead. So far, we have seen very little of that kind of thought in the state legislatures. My major concern is simply that, as we proceed along this road, we comprehend the full dimensions of the risk. This conviction leads me to urge that state legislatures not endorse the budget convention campaign on the basis of over-confident answers to unanswered and unanswerable questions, or of blithe statements that inadvertently or intentionally blind us to the genuine hazards.

The Meaning of Article V

Charles L. Black, Jr.

I think the best thing to do is to get down and consider exactly what, right now, we are really talking about. I am holding a resolution, which I believe to be fairly typical, passed by the Senate and the House of the state of Kansas. The first section—and this is fairly important—provides that the legislature of Kansas is petitioning the Congress to pass an amendment and submit it to the states, an amendment which would require that within five years after its ratification by the various states, in the absence of a national emergency, the total of all appropriations made by Congress for a fiscal year shall not exceed the total of all estimated federal revenues for such fiscal year. And here we come to the part that interests us today—"and be it further resolved that alternatively, the legislature of the State of Kansas hereby makes application to the Congress of the United States to call a convention for the sole and exclusive purpose of proposing an amendment to the Constitution of the United States, which would require that in the absence of a national emergency, the total of all appropriations made by the Congress for a fiscal year shall not exceed the total of all estimated federal revenues for such year."

Now, although there is a certain variation among the applications, I think it is fair to say that enough of them are of this form, or approximately this form, or of a form logically similar to this, that we can say we would not be here today if we knew that all the applications, so worded and based on such a theory, were invalid and did not ask for the thing that Article V authorizes the states to ask for—and to get, upon thirty-four of them asking for it. The theory of the Kansas resolution, typical as it is, is that Article V means that the thing the states can ask for is a convention for the purpose—and here I hesitate a little because this is what they said and not I—of proposing, not even of considering, but of *proposing*. Consider that they insist on that phraseology even though objection has been made to it, at least by me, for sixteen years, from youth to old age.

And "of proposing"—and then there is given an amendment in particularized detail, complete detail. The difference between that and direct quotation is merely trivial. It is a description of an amendment, all the operative parts of which are put there by the legislature of Kansas, for the sole and exclusive purpose of proposing—or, let us grant for the sake of argument, of considering whether to propose—*this one amendment.*

There are two different views, different though one includes the other and they are not contradictory, which I have put forward on the meaning of Article V. One of them is—and I stand by it and I am ready to defend it at any time—that Article V meant a general convention, a convention for proposing amendments, such amendments as that convention might see fit to propose. Of course, if that were the correct interpretation, or were taken to be the correct interpretation, there would be no problem about any of these calls. The other, a narrower view within that view, or at least a circle within it, is that at the least, Article V does not mean a convention—a solemn convention of dignitaries, presumably able people, summoned from all over the country—for the purpose of voting yes or no on a proposal, which, in every colloquial sense of the word "propose," has already been "proposed" by the state of Kansas. The state of Kansas has carefully said, as though to forestall the efforts of those who would find a "general equity" or a "cy pres," or something of the sort, that the convention is to be for the "*sole and exclusive* purpose of proposing" this amendment.

It is a long uphill scramble to convert that into a call for a convention to deal generally with the problem of anxiety about fiscal expenditures. They tell us exactly what they want, and they tell us that is all they want, and they use the characteristic English pleonasm (a doublet) "sole and exclusive" to make sure that we know this is really *all* that they want us to do.

I am glad that I do not have the job of devising the set of words that will convert that petition into a request for a kind of general budget-balancing convention, which might consider such things as whether to spend more on medical care, or whether to withhold funds from all the schools that pray, or from all the schools that do not pray, or any of those questions. I think they are all questions that have to do with the spending of money.

There is just one thing, and I think we ought to keep it in mind, because it is what faces us right now: whether this petition and others like it constitute applications for the thing for which Article V authorizes the states to apply. I would think that the question whether an application is valid, or whether the convention it calls for is the type of convention meant by the language of Article V, ought to be the same question. Otherwise, we have the situation where—and I think Lester Orfield accepted this in his book without quite seeing the difficulties of

11

it—the applications would force the call of a convention, but then the convention could not be limited.

That seems to me a poor kind of law. If the convention really cannot be limited, then an illimitable convention is the thing that the states have to ask for. Otherwise, we would be fatally drawn into a runaway situation without anybody at any time wishing this—except the members of the convention who are actually going to run away.

Now, as to what this Article V language means, there is nothing harder than dealing with plain language. The question of what five or six words mean is, of course, a question on which people can always differ. But I prefer to take this Article V language—"a convention for proposing amendments"—and place it in the procedural context in which we anticipate it will be used, and to do with it what lawyers sometimes do with language in a statute or other authoritative document: attribute legal effect to language and to the events to which that language refers, and track the statute. So I can imagine an application from the state of Kansas that says, "The legislature of the state of Kansas hereby makes application to the Congress of the United States to call a convention for the purpose of proposing amendments." Now that would track Article V. That is what Article V says, and I cannot see how one could ask anything but two questions about that language in such an application.

First, would the application be valid? I understand there are some people who think that it would not, and this was apparently the view of Senator Ervin in his bill, because he provided—and maybe Senator Helms's bill does again—that you *must* apply for a limited convention, otherwise the application will not be received. I do not understand that view. I cannot believe that, on reflection and on one's attention being called to the difficulty of the point, a lawyer would say that an application that actually tracks the Constitution and uses the words of the Article themselves, *ipsissimis verbis,* is not valid because it fails to insert a limitation that the Constitution does not insert. The other question is, if it is *valid*, then what would it *mean* as it stands, in this valid application? Plainly, again, is it not so that it *must* mean a convention for proposing such amendments as the convention decides to propose?

If I am right about both those points, then we have at least transferred the issue a little. We can perceive that *one* of the plain meanings, the meaning which the language would bear in the context in which it is used if it were used alone, is "a general convention for proposing amendments." That is a valuable transfer of emphasis if we buy it, and if we do not, I would be interested in knowing why. But if we buy it, then we have to ask whether any given addition of another type of convention, qualitatively different—as different from this convention as is the freedom to marry and the freedom to marry one of two or three people designated by somebody else—is also included within language that can bear a very important and significant plain meaning all its own without any addition. The question that faces the United States, and will face the Congress if these things come up to Congress, is this. Is there enough reason—reason in history, reason in lexicography, reason, above all, in the master canon of constitutional construction, which is imputing or finding the intent (usually undiscoverable) of the people in Philadelphia—to consider valid an application which is for the sole and exclusive purpose of convening a convention that is to consider whether or not to propose a certain amendment, an amendment which is as good as quoted in the Kansas resolution and in some other resolutions?

I believe that there is not, I am sure that there is not, in the history of the thing, any evidence sufficient to establish this meaning. I think the master canon of construction I have mentioned tends just the other way. And it is preposterous to think that what is meant by this language, among other things, is a misuse of Article V just as Henry VIII misused the *congé d'elire*—namely, only the bishop that Henry VIII chose to designate.

The Case for a General Constitutional Convention

Laurence H. Silberman

I started out in sympathy with the notion of attempting to deal with macroeconomic problems through a constitutional convention. However, I have been persuaded by the wisdom of Professor Black's view that a limited convention is absolutely impossible; it is not contemplated by the Constitution. I am not persuaded, though, by his corollary position that any application coming from a state legislature is void if it specifies a subject to be dealt with by the convention.

I too would be troubled about an application that uses the language "sole and exclusive purpose," as the Kansas resolution does. That application is probably void. But I am more persuaded by Professor Gunther's view that simply mentioning subjects, one or more, that a state wishes the convention to take up can be appropriately considered the grounds which generate the call. And there is a reason why that is important.

Congress must determine when it has a contemporaneous call from two-thirds of the states. The quality of being contemporary, in my view, can be expressed in two ways. One is by time. If all the applications arrive in Washington on the same day with the language that Professor Black describes as tracking the constitution exactly, we clearly have a contemporaneous call. On the other hand, if the applications arrive at different times but refer to a similar subject, this fact should be considered by Congress in determining whether there has been a contemporaneous call. In any event, I believe that determination will be a political question for Congress and that it will not be subject to judicial review.

But let me answer Professor Gunther's challenge. He says—and I think correctly—that one should not seek a constitutional convention lightly. It would be, after all, an unlimited convention, and if state legislatures call for it, they must have in mind something broader than one issue if that one issue is not of transcendental importance.

I have come to the view that a general convention would now be appropriate, useful, and proper, and I should like to express the theme of such a convention, and some of the issues I think it would take up.

Our Constitution, developed in 1787, was fundamentally directed toward the limitation of governmental power. But in fact, many of the limitations it sought to place upon governmental power have since been frustrated for all sorts of reasons. A new convention could very well be called with an overall theme of reducing governmental power, that is, the power of the executive, the independent agencies, and the judiciary.

There are also some more specific issues, in particular, how to deal with macroeconomic questions. Whether phrased in terms of budget balancing or spending limitations, Professor Laurence Tribe, and to a certain extent Professor Gunther, have suggested that these questions are not of transcendental importance. Professor Tribe makes the argument that, after all, we all thought it was wrong when the Supreme Court tried to write its own views of economic theory into the Constitution. Therefore, he leaps to the conclusion that it would be a mistake for the United States to seek to deal with macroeconomics through a constitutional amendment, even though macroeconomic questions have as a corollary questions of the size of government.

There is a hole in that argument. The great intellectual debate among and within the industrial democracies is between the democratic socialists and the democratic capitalists, and it turns on one fundamental question: Does political liberty depend, to a certain extent, or perhaps entirely, on a degree of economic liberty?

If one takes the view that political freedom does depend on economic freedom, then one must conclude that it is perfectly appropriate under our Constitution to call a convention, in part, to consider the degree of economic liberty, which is another way of phrasing the degree to which the government can appropriate money from its citizens for, among other purposes, the redistribution of income.

With regard to Congress itself, a political scientist, Morris Fiorina, published a brilliant book entitled *Congress: Keystone of the Washington Establishment* (Yale University Press, 1977). Fiorina's theory is that there has been a fundamental change, particularly accelerated over the last twenty or thirty years, in the way in which Congress does its business. The professionalization of congressmen and the fact that each becomes an ombudsman with a vested interest in the growth of governmental power reduce Congress's viability as a policy-making body.

This suggests to me that it is perfectly appropriate for a constitutional convention to consider a limit on congressional terms, particularly in the House. Also, I would suggest an amendment to elaborate the dormant view expressed by the Supreme Court in *Schechter Poultry:* that Congress cannot delegate legislative power to the executive or anybody else. That kind of provision would go a long way to preclude the expansion of government, and it seems to me quite appropriate to consider.

Next, I have come to the view that the independent regulatory agencies are a constitutional anomaly and should be eliminated. Their function should be taken into the executive branch. I had a fascinating experience when six of us—three Democrats and three Republicans and, roughly speaking, three liberals and three conservatives—went down to advise the governor of the Virgin Islands on a new constitution. At one point, the governor asked what they should put in the constitution regarding independent regulatory agencies. And, unanimously, we all said, "Preclude them." We were all of the view that these agencies have grown like Topsy, unresponsive to political will, and that all their functions, apart from adjudication, should be in the executive branch, where they would be responsive to political will. This is especially true of the agencies' policy-making functions. If we had a convention today, this would be an important issue for it to consider.

But the social issues, sometimes referred to pejoratively as the single-interest issues, may be the most important of current constitutional concerns. (These issues all involve implicit attacks on judicial activism.) Let us take the establishment clause of the First Amendment. Future historians looking back on the United States 500 years from today may well say that our rigorous antireligious interpretation of the establishment clause as it has developed over the previous 30 years has been more important in terms of American history than our economic problems. Can anyone say that the way we treat religion as a single issue is an unimportant question?

How about abortion? Those who refer to that as a single issue are basically people who believe in abortion. My own views, as a policy matter, track the Supreme Court's abortion decision, although I am appalled that the Court decided that case as a matter of constitutional law. How we deal with abortion seems to me, in philosophic-political terms, to be no less important than how we dealt with slavery or murder. And I contend that a constitutional amendment that leaves the law on abortion to the states would be singularly appropriate because there is no national consensus on that issue.

Another such question is equality of opportunity, rather than equality of result, and the corollary issue of desegregation, rather than integration. The decisions of administrative agencies and courts on affirmative action over the last twenty years seem to me to challenge the basic ideology of American democracy. Who can say that a constitutional convention that considers affirmative action and related questions would be dealing with a frivolous question, a single issue? Professor Tribe has said that a convention should not deal with these questions because the Constitution should express fundamental enduring national values. But in what sense are these *not* issues that reflect fundamental enduring national values?

16

What are the risks of an unlimited convention? I agree with Professor Gunther that the potential risk is that some of these proposals I mention would be approved by a convention and then adopted by three-quarters of the states. But I find that not a risk.

Some people, particularly journalists, are worried that the convention might challenge the other part of the First Amendment, the free speech clause. In that respect, I wish to point out that the original constitutional convention expressed views that sprang from the American experience, not views that came down from Mt. Sinai. I do not think it a real possibility that anyone would seek to repeal the free speech clause or any of the other important guarantees of the Bill of Rights. There is just not a respectable body of opinion in this country to weaken the Bill of Rights.

What about problems of conflict between Congress and the convention? I see no such problems, assuming that Congress does not seek to limit the activities of the convention, which, I agree totally with Professor Black, it cannot do. It may try, but that is a risk we must run. I view Congress's role as limited to calling the convention and providing for the selection of delegates. On the latter point, Congress has some options and they will be fiercely debated, because the method of selecting delegates may well have an impact on the personality of the convention, although in my judgment not as much as some would think.

Finally, on the question of divisiveness, I am reminded of my grandfather's description of Franklin D. Roosevelt. He disliked everything Roosevelt did, and every time he mentioned Roosevelt to me when I was only a little boy, he would describe him as a divisive influence in American politics. And what he meant by divisive—it took me a number of years to understand—was that Roosevelt had 60 percent.

The Origins of Article V
of the Constitution

Gordon S. Wood

I am delighted to be here on this panel with all these distinguished legal and constitutional scholars. Since eighteenth-century historians are not usually asked to participate in discussions of current public issues, I am not sure of my role. I do have personal views about the advisability or wisdom of calling a constitutional convention, but I do not want to argue them here. Instead, I would like to put the issue into a historical framework and raise a few questions. I would like to talk a little about the Constitutional Convention of 1787 and the origins of the amending process.

Our legal and constitutional tradition is very peculiar. From the very beginning we have had a tendency to reduce complicated political questions to legal or constitutional ones. One thinks immediately of the most embarrassing example of this: the attempt by the Supreme Court in 1857 to head off sectional conflict over slavery with the *Dred Scott* decision. But that is only the most conspicuous example. Our entire history is filled with such efforts to solve political problems through judicial determinations and through interpretations of the Constitution, often resting on the framers' intent. The Constitution is our biblical authority, the supreme text against which we measure what we do or want to do. It is the final resting place for political disputes, the floor that keeps us from falling into a bottomless pit of democratic squabbling. And it has been that from the beginning of the nation's history.

The ink was scarcely dry on the Constitution before disputes arose over the intentions of the framers. In the ratifying conventions, those who had been at the Philadelphia Convention were given a distinct status. They spoke with a special authority, for they presumably knew what the intent of the framers was. Elbridge Gerry, who had been at the Philadelphia Convention, was defeated for election to the Massachusetts ratifying convention. But the delegates invited him anyway to sit on the sidelines. He was not allowed to debate or vote, but he could answer questions of fact. Right away people wanted to know what the framers intended by this provision or that.

Given this immediate obsession with the intentions of the Founding

Fathers, it is particularly ironic that the fullest and most reliable source of what went on at Philadelphia—Madison's notes of the debates—was not published until 1840, more than a half-century after the convention met. That should tell us something about the peculiar character of our fascination with the intentions of the Founding Fathers. We really do not want to know what the actual intentions of the framers were in 1787. Nor should we want these actual intentions to be the basis of our legal and constitutional system. Madison certainly knew what revealing the actual intentions could do, which is why he withheld publishing his notes until after his death. Publication, he said in 1821, "should be delayed till the Constitution should be well settled by practice and till a knowledge of the controversial part of the proceedings of its framers could be turned to no improper account." In fact, to the end of his life Madison kept trying to direct attention away from the intent of the Philadelphia Convention toward the intent of the state ratifying conventions as the only authoritative source for interpreting the Constitution.

Madison had a good reason for this ploy, for the state ratifying conventions were open public affairs; their debates were published almost at once, sometimes in newspapers, and consequently the delegates never said anything in them that was antidemocratic. But the Philadelphia Convention was very different, and that difference ought to give pause to those who say we could duplicate what those men did in Philadelphia two hundred years ago. The delegates to the Philadelphia Convention took extraordinary measures to keep their proceedings private: they took vows of secrecy; no copies of anything in the journal were allowed; nothing said in the convention was to be released or communicated to the outside society; and sentries were even posted to keep out intruders. Try to imagine a constitutional convention today getting away with that! Naturally the press complained, as did Jefferson from Paris. Even his friend Madison would not tell him the details of what was going on.

The secrecy at Philadelphia made a difference. The debates there were remarkably bold and candid, particularly when compared with those of the ratifying conventions in the states. In the closed Philadelphia Convention many delegates were willing to discuss sensitive issues like aristocracy and the fear of popular power in ways they were not able to several months later in the open ratifying conventions. Madison reportedly said later that "no Constitution would ever have been adopted by the convention if the debates had been public." Many of the Founding Fathers were not at all happy with the spread of democracy since the Revolution and were in fact trying to create a structure that might mitigate some of democracy's evil effects. For them democracy was still a problem to be solved; it had not yet become the article of faith that it is for us.

The point of all this is that the historically recovered intentions of the framers may not be the intentions our jurists want or need. To many historians it seems clear that our obsession with the intentions of the framers is a convention, a fiction, a device we use to make our constitutional system work. Historical recovery of the actual intentions of the Founding Fathers would undoubtedly work against the legal and constitutional interpretive process—which is why most of our jurists have never been good historians: authentic understanding of the past would undermine what they do.

Still, it might be worthwhile for a historian to say something about the origins of Article V. It is an interesting story.

The need for some sort of special amending process grew out of the new meaning Americans had given to a constitution in the Revolution. If a written constitution was an extraordinary, fundamental kind of law, different from ordinary statutory legislation, then some way of changing that law other than the ordinary lawmaking process was necessary. Many of the states had wrestled with this problem in the years since 1776 and had experimented with several devices for changing their new revolutionary state constitutions. Six states did nothing and left the legislatures free to alter their constitutions through legislation. But the other seven states had various amending processes. Delaware required a five-sevenths majority of the Assembly for constitutional alterations. The Maryland constitution could be changed by the acts of two successive, separately elected legislatures. But by the early 1780s the new constitutions of Massachusetts and New Hampshire had developed the notion of holding special constitutional conventions—bodies distinct from the regular legislature that met for the sole purpose of writing or changing the constitution.

It was this new idea of a convention that the creators of the Philadelphia Convention drew upon, both for their own meeting and eventually for Article V. But providing for a means of altering the Constitution they were writing was not something most delegates cared to think about too much. This explains the confused, offhand, and belated manner in which Article V was put together.

The Virginia plan had referred to the need for some sort of amending process that did not involve Congress. In the discussion of the issue on June 5, some delegates objected to bypassing Congress. Action was postponed to June 10 when similar objections were raised to leaving Congress out. By now it was clear that the delegates who wanted Congress excluded from a role in the amending process were precisely those least attracted to the emerging new and powerful national government, particularly Elbridge Gerry and George Mason. On July 23 the convention decided to provide for some sort of amending process, but not exclude Congress from a central role in it. On August 6 the Committee of Detail reported a provision stating that on the application of two-thirds of the state legislatures, Congress shall call a convention. During the debate on this provision on September 10, several delegates raised objections. Madison in particular was worried about the whole idea of a convention. He could see in it a latent threat to the work then going on in Philadelphia, and he raised in the debates the same kinds of questions that are being asked today: How would a convention be formed? What would be its procedures? and so on.

Then followed a number of amendments, including a suggestion by Roger Sherman that Congress could also propose amendments to the states for their consent. James Wilson first tried to lessen the need for the unanimous consent of the states to an amendment by suggesting that only two-thirds of the states need consent. When this failed, he suggested three-fourths, which passed.

At this point Madison saw an opportunity to bring off a legislative coup. Everyone was sufficiently confused by the discussion and the piling up of amendments on top of one another that he shrewdly proposed shelving the existing provision and substituting a completely new one. His new provision did what he and other nationalists wanted to do all along, which was to eliminate entirely the idea of a convention as a means of amendment. His proposal gave Congress responsibility to propose amendments either on its own authority or upon application of two-thirds of the states, followed by ratification of such amendments by three-fourths of the states. Hamilton seconded the proposal and it passed 9 to 1.

That was how matters stood until September 15, when the Committee of Style reported this article. This was two days before the convention adjourned. Sherman added the provision that the states may not lose their equal votes in the Senate. Then suddenly George Mason woke up. He must have been out to lunch or dozing five days earlier when Madison had made his fast switch. He now thought that the chairman of the Committee of Style, Gouverneur Morris, had pulled a fast one and had made the change. Mason argued that Congress could not be left with sole authority to make amendments. It was too self-interested and would become oppressive. He thus proposed that Congress be required to call a convention on application of two-thirds of the states.

One can imagine Madison's chagrin. He had almost slipped his article through. He again raised all sorts of objections to the idea of a convention; but he could not make too much of a fuss without further

21

arousing the suspicions of his nationalist intentions among many delegates. There was no point in endangering what had been gained for the sake of the amending process.

Yet Madison had good reason to fear the convention mode of amendment. Once the Constitution was made public, its opponents began talking about a second national convention to amend it. The Federalists spent a lot of their energy in the subsequent months trying to talk people out of such a second convention. It would, said Washington, "set everything afloat again." Several of the states ratified with the expectation that there would be another convention, and North Carolina refused to ratify precisely because they anticipated a new convention. A second convention became the basis of the Anti-Federalist strategy.

The convention was thus a political weapon in 1787–1788, and it has remained one ever since. But because it has never been used at the national level, it has a kind of doomsday machine quality about it: no one can be quite sure what invoking a convention would mean.

Yet the historical experience is not such a void as we first might think. There have been lots of constitutional conventions in American history—at the state level. Unfortunately, we do not know a great deal about how they operated. Perhaps because of this ignorance and the uncertainty flowing from it, both the proponents and opponents of a new national convention have not been much interested in invoking this state experience.

There is no denying the importance of constitutional conventions for the states. The convention has become the major means of amending a constitution and in fact is the only mode of constitutional revision common to all fifty states. Since the beginning of our national history, there have been about 220 state constitutional conventions. The state legislatures have played a wide variety of roles in all of them. Some of the conventions have been limited to specific issues; others have been unlimited. Of the thirty state constitutional conventions between 1938 and 1975, twelve were limited and eighteen were unlimited. In all this state experience there are precedents galore for whatever argument one wants to make.

Yet precisely because the states have been so free and easy in calling conventions, their experience may not be what anyone wants to draw upon. The state constitutions generally have been very changeable and long-winded documents. There have been about 140 different state constitutions in two hundred years, and the 50 state constitutions have been amended nearly 5,000 times. Their average length is at least three times as long as the federal Constitution; their average age is about ninety years. Since 1812 Louisiana has had twelve different constitutions. The Georgia constitution has over 650 amendments.

If we are not to use this state experience, then we are left with a very vague, empty, and permissive situation that seems to allow momentous consequences to flow from a technical provision of the Constitution that is not part of our national experience. It is this peculiar situation that seems to account for the emotions aroused by a move to call a national convention. Opponents are alarmed that a series of relatively isolated, even parochial, decisions in the separate states could add up to something that was never adequately discussed and deliberated at a national level. The convention procedure appears anachronistic to many; it seems to do violence to the way we have come to conduct our national politics. The problem it has created graphically illustrates the vastly different role the states now play in our political affairs and in our consciousness from the role they were expected to play at the end of the eighteenth century.

It is for this reason that I do not think a national convention is likely, not unless our national leaders, influenced by pressure at the national level, decide that one is needed. Without this national agreement I do not think we will have a convention even if two-thirds of the states do apply to the Congress for one. Congress can always find excuses to disallow the necessary state applications. What all this shows, I suppose, is that there are limits to what a rather brief document written nearly two hundred years ago can be expected to do in providing the framework for a great nation's political business.

Thoughts on the Value
of the Convention Alternative

Paul M. Bator

I am very much of a kindergarten child on this issue, because I followed it only in the most casual way until very recently, when I read a short piece by Professor Bruce Ackerman of Yale in the *New Republic*. That article got me sufficiently enraged so that I became really interested and devoted some study to the issue. Later, I discovered that Professor Ackerman was merely giving a trendy version of a more thoughtful but equally enraging position held by Professor Black.

Let me try to sharpen the distinction between the positions of Professors Gunther and Black. As I understand it, Professor Gunther's view is that we cannot be certain that there is any effective way of limiting a convention to a single subject or a single proposal, that there is considerable doubt whether the states and the Congress, even acting in tandem, have the constitutional power to limit the convention. Further, he adds, even if in theory they have the power, there is doubt whether there is any effective way of enforcing that power and ensuring that the limitation will hold.

Professor Black's position seems to me to be profoundly different. It is that the convention method of amendment provided for in Article V is simply inapposite and unavailable for the purpose of addressing a specific or limited shortcoming in the Constitution. Apparently his view is that the convention method has only one function: to address a total revision of the Constitution. If the states see a *specific* shortcoming in the Constitution and call for a convention for the purpose of addressing that specific shortcoming, the call is totally illegitimate and, indeed, Congress is simply to ignore it. It is to ignore any call for a convention that is addressed to less than a total or unlimited rewrite because it is illegal, because Article V, substantively, simply does not make the convention method available as a way of dealing with specific issues and specific amendments.

I see these two positions as different not just in content but also in spirit. What Professor Gunther is telling us is that if thirty-four states perceive, in common, that there is some deep, but specific, shortcoming in the existing constitutional plan, then it is legitimate for the states, if

24

Congress does not act on its own, to try to use the convention method to address that shortcoming. What Professor Gunther says, however, is that this is a risky thing to do, that it should be done, therefore, only with very, very great concern; because there is no way of ensuring that the institution which is set up to deal with that issue and that shortcoming will not then go all over the place and try to deal with everything else, too. I am not sure that I agree with this, but it is what I would call a legitimate constitutional concern. It raises the question whether the institutional scheme created by the Constitution is well designed for dealing with specific constitutional concerns.

Professor Black's interpretation, I must say, strikes me as profoundly anticonstitutional. In fact, I thought the most revealing thing Professor Black did was that, when he started, he read that resolution from one of the states, and made a slip of the tongue and said, "the state of Congress has passed the following resolution." I think he meant "Kansas." That seems to me a profoundly Freudian slip. What Professor Black's view does is to ignore the central concern to which the convention alternative of Article V was directed.

And in spite of Professor Wood's caution here, I do think one gets from the language, from the contemporaneous accounts, from *The Federalist Papers,* and from the ratification debates, a sense of what concerns animated the framers in trying to design this structure. The central concern was simply that there ought to be some recourse if intransigent central authority adamantly refuses to correct, or to allow to be put in play the forces for correcting, a deeply felt constitutional insufficiency or flaw. And there is absolutely nothing in the words or in the history of Article V to suggest that its convention-calling option is simply unavailable if that central governmental intransigence relates to something specific, or indeed to anything short of the total constitutional plan.

What Professor Black's interpretation tells us is this: if the central government—and by that I mean Congress and the Supreme Court—are in agreement on a constitutional position on a specific issue, then, even though that is widely unacceptable, there is just nothing under Article V that the states and the people can do about it, unless they hide the fact that what they object to is a specific constitutional position. They must somehow pretend that what they want is an unlimited all-purpose convention. If, for instance, Congress passes a statute that allows the FBI to censor mail and the Supreme Court says that that is constitutional, there is simply no way we can deal with that, unless the states deal with it by pretending that what they want is a convention for rewriting the entire Constitution.

I submit that there is nothing in Article V, or its history, which suggests that the convention method is to be deemed illegitimate whenever the states wish to *amend*—as against totally rewriting—the Constitution. In fact, the very statement of the position suggests how bizarre it is. What Professor Black is really saying is that the convention method is apposite only if what we are interested in is *not* an amendment or amendments but, rather, a total reconsideration of the entire document.

I think that the issues can best be framed if we think of this in a specific setting. Suppose that thirty-four resolutions arrive, and some group, say, the Senate Judiciary Committee, must consider whether this is a valid call for a convention and must decide what Congress's role is to be. Here again the central issue is the spirit in which this is done. Will it be a spirit of generosity and hospitality toward the underlying purposes of the constitutional structure?

Professor Black, I think, would invalidate a lot of those petitions. And it is true that they do have problems. They differ in minor ways: some are conditional; and there are all kinds of other problems with them. But the mood in which Professor Black faces those petitions reminds me of nothing so much as the way in which, one gathers, literacy tests were administered at the polls in the South in the 1910s and 1920s: unless every *t* is crossed, and every *i* is dotted, they were simply thrown out.

I agree much more with Professor Gunther's spirit on this. The resolutions ought to be seen as expressing a common concern directed at a certain *group* of issues. At this point, though, I depart a little from Professor Gunther. I agree that we cannot guarantee a limited convention. Article V is opaque; in its structural details, it is silent. But the one thing that a sensible and a generous interpretation makes clear is that there must somehow be a sharing or a partnership between the "calling" states, the Congress, and the convention itself in creating the ground rules for what the convention is to do and how it is to operate. There is no way out of that.

I do not understand why we should decide in advance that we cannot and should not try to limit the area covered by the convention. We cannot be certain that it will work, but we cannot be certain that it will not. If Congress, for instance, says that the existing resolutions betoken a concern with the issue of the level of federal expenditures, the level of income, and the relations between them, and that *that* is all the convention should address, then Congress is legitimately doing exactly what Article V contemplates, which is giving play to the concerns that led to the call for the convention. And that, in turn, places enormous political and moral pressures on the convention not to wander far afield. We cannot be sure that it will not get out of hand and deal with a whole lot of other subjects, but if we try conscientiously to create a kind of partnership structure, then the process has a dynamic of its own. And

I think it would be politically very difficult for a convention, at that point, to turn to issues like abortion or others.

I do agree with Professor Gunther that it is a risk. And I think that Mr. Silberman is far too complacent in envisioning an unlimited convention: he just assumes that it will be a libertarian convention. But the convention is not going to happen today; it is going to happen, if it does happen, some time in the future, and we do not know what the politics will be then. We do not have just little old people with tennis shoes from the right wing; we have little old people with tennis shoes from the left wing, too. And we may end up with a left-wing, interventionist, egalitarian convention.

The risk exists. Professor Wood is right that this is an untried institution, but I disagree with the tenor of his words to the effect that Article V creates a technical, outdated, and archaic kind of process or structure. I think the Article V convention represents a profound political protection for us, as a people, against the tyranny of central government. And whatever we say about Article V, I think it is very, very wrong, just because we may disagree with the content of any particular constitutional amendment that is now being proposed, to interpret Article V in such a way as to clip its wings as a protection for the liberties of the people.

That is why I think it is profoundly important, particularly for constitutional scholars, to be hospitable toward the concern that Article V represents, which is that there be a way out for the states and the people if a willful and intransigent central authority governs us in a way that we find unacceptable.

Discussion

PROFESSOR GROVER REES, University of Texas Law School: I would like the panelists to comment on two contentions of mine that derive from a historical study I have done in another area of the amending process. I submit that an important reason why Article V is so brief is not that the framers expected Congress or somebody else to fill in the details, but that they expected that the common understanding of contract law (particularly as it had been applied in international law over the years, since they regarded the Constitution as a compact among sovereigns) would be applied. That is not an infusion of one area of the law into another because contract law is just a simple way of deciding when people have agreed on something. In this context, I conclude that the power to propose something, absent express or clearly implied limitations, includes the power to limit it. Therefore, if a state may call, with thirty-three other states, for an unlimited convention, it may also call for a limited convention.

Professor Black's indictment of the Kansas resolution is that it precludes a necessary thirty-four-state consensus. To take a much simpler example, several states have called for a right-to-life convention. Thirteen are saying that a convention could consider amendments similar to such-and-such, or consider amendments on the right-to-life. Mississippi's, however, is very explicit and has an exception for rape. If you apply my view, a convention called by thirty-four states, one of which is Mississippi, is precluded by its call from considering an amendment that does not exclude the case of rape.

Applying this to the Kansas resolution, a convention could result from thirty-four identical calls, but all it could do is consider that Kansas resolution. On the other hand, if you have that Kansas resolution and another different "solely-and-exclusively" resolution containing the Milton Friedman amendment, Congress should properly ignore them.

Second, I think the application of contract law implies Supreme Court review. *Coleman* v. *Miller* notwithstanding, the function of the Supreme Court is to say what the law is—what the Constitution contains. Moreover, there is very little evidence that, aside from certain substantive powers the Congress has in the amending process, Congress was intended to have any role in adjudicating questions about that process. In other words, would it not be feasible to apply contract law with Supreme Court review—or, perhaps, even during the convention process by declaratory judgment in the form of, "Yes, you have amended the Constitution," or, "No, you have not"?

PROFESSOR BLACK: The question whether contract law is applicable is very difficult. A number of the members of the 1787 convention, perhaps including Madison, contrasted the Constitution's coming into effect with a contract or compact, and that is why they wanted to submit it to conventions rather than to the state legislatures, because they feared that it might be looked on as a compact with various consequences. The main thing is that this speaks to the issue of hospitality. When we look at the hospitality to be accorded to Kansas, it is a hospitality that says, "Come right on in but leave your left leg behind." It is a highly selective hospitality that is hospitable only to what we want you to bring in, but not to your very clearly expressed desire that that is absolutely all that you want this convention to be called for. You misunderstood my position about validity, I'm afraid. I think thirty-four applications such as the Kansas one would all be invalid, one by one.

And as for illiteracy, it seems to me that Professor Bator attributes a profound illiteracy to the state of Kansas—that they just do not know how to say what they mean, and that they use words like *sole* and *exclusive* without meaning them at all. They have just written them in automatically, and our job is to disregard them.

As for the Supreme Court, I think much too much has been read into *Coleman* v. *Miller,* and the Supreme Court should have responsibility in these things. But, I would not rate the odds very high that the Court will take on such a case.

PROFESSOR GUNTHER: I do not want to comment on the general relevance of contract law, but the question does bring several things to mind. First, whatever contract law says, Charles Black implies, if Kansas were the prototype of all thirty-four applications, the states would be calling for a convention that would simply be an occasion for an up-and-down vote on a specific proposal. And after talking earlier about how much uncertainty there is, I should add that the only constitutional issue that I find every scholar agreeing on is that such a convention simply is *not* a convention. That would be a rubber stamp, not a convention, and that is not what the Constitution contemplates.

As for judical review, both the Ervin bill and the Helms bill very explicitly—and, I think, somewhat questionably—go out of their way to say, "No judicial review of anything; Congress is final." That result certainly is not required by the political question cases such as *Coleman v. Miller.*

But a broader point comes to mind on the contract law issue. I do not remember much contract law, thank God, but I think one notion that runs through it is that people on both sides—the various participants in a deal—ought to have a general sense of a common understanding of what they are talking about. But in the present process, the varying assumptions at large—in the state legislatures; the half-baked, incoherent assumptions by various people in Congress; and the unknown assumptions of a future convention—constitute nothing resembling a meeting of the minds.

Now, what does that failure to agree on assumptions suggest? Earlier, I blasted the state legislatures for being irresponsible in voting for a convention with most of them not thinking about what they were really voting for. I ought to add, in terms of the potential "contracting" parties, that I think Congress is being similarly irresponsible. I think it is outrageous—putting aside Congress's political motivations for not wanting to confront this issue—that we have this kind of cloud of uncertainty over the convention process. We could and should understand more about it, and Congress could surely help dispel the doubts. Why doesn't the Senate Judiciary Committee hold hearings along the lines of the kind of discussion we are having here? We should know whether a substantial number of people would agree, for example, with my position that you can have a subject specification in a congressional call, but that it is only a moral exhortation and that a convention can go beyond congressional specifications in its deliberations. In my view, the ultimate scope of a convention turns to a large extent on the political dynamics during the election of delegates. Why doesn't Congress air that view, which I think is widely shared? That airing would inform state legislators so that they could consider rescinding or saying that this is the kind of convention process they truly want to get into. The only thing I think to be truly intolerable is the present process, where state legislators do not think about it and where Congress has not done a thing to help inform them.

If Congress turned its attention to the substantive problems at least, they might do some things far more useful than the present sporadic enterprises on the Hill—for example, the Mickey Mousing process by some senators of taking each application in turn and finding technical flaws in it. Some of the technical flaws I have heard suggested seem to me nothing more than bizarre, old-fashioned contract and pleading law. What Congress really ought to be doing instead is helping clear the air. Behave like a responsible political body, at least: listen to people, and even if they want to vote politically on what their sense of the understanding is, that would at least help inform the states of what they are getting under way by voting for a convention. Some deliberate congressional attention to these issues might in fact help us understand more clearly what would be at stake in the delegate election process, and what a convention might legitimately talk about when it does convene.

I would add this: I, personally, think that a lot of things in the Helms bill are of highly questionable constitutionality. But the Helms bill is sitting there, just as the Ervin bill sat there more than a decade ago and was approved by the Senate with overwhelming votes but without serious discussion, except in one hearing in 1967. In short, I think that, in addition to blasting the state legislatures for their irresponsibility, we ought to blast our Republicans and Democrats on the judiciary committees of both houses, and the Congress as a whole, for being as totally inattentive and therefore contemptuous of the constitutional scheme as I think they are being right now.

BRUCE BARTLETT, Office of Senator Roger Jepson: On the question of the validity of applications and who is going to make the decision, it seems to me quite obvious that the Senate Judiciary Committee will probably have some opportunity to vote on it. Does the House Judiciary Committee also enter into this process? What if the two judiciary committees disagree on various applications? Will this eventually come up before the entire Senate or the entire House for a vote? And is there any possibility of judicial review? If an application is deemed invalid, what happens if a state quickly decides to pass another resolution right away? And are there time limits on these applications?

PROFESSOR BLACK: Part of this is really not controversial. There must be, ultimately, one vote, at least, in Congress. The Congress is to call a convention, and that vote, presumably, would be influenced, and should be totally influenced, by Congress's perception of where the right lies as between me and other people, like Professor Bator. It is, in a sense, a political decision, but I think it is a legal question to the extent that Congress has to decide whether, as a matter of law, the applications are valid. Nobody else can do that at this initial stage, obviously.

As to judicial review, I think that many of us think there should be more judicial review of constitutional amendment provisions than is actually foreshadowed by the leading case of *Coleman* v. *Miller*. I think that case has been overinterpreted, but that is the kind of uncertainty that we have. We know that many people are putting the case forward as committing *all* the questions to Congress. I do not think that

31

is right. But as Professor Gunther points out, the bills now pending would do that to an extent that is quite alarming.

PROFESSOR BATOR: The present balanced budget campaign, if one assumes those applications are all addressed to the same issue, really does not raise a problem of contemporaneousness. They are all within the last three or four years.

PROFESSOR BLACK: I certainly agree with that.

MR. SILBERMAN: I am very troubled by the notion of judicial review in this area. As much as I would like to see a constitutional convention, I would not like to see it at the price of judicial intervention in what I think is necessarily a political decision by Congress. There are no limitations in the Constitution which define contemporaneousness. And contemporaneousness, both of time and subject, is a political question that has to be decided by Congress voting as a whole.

I fully recognize that many congressmen will be motivated by a spirit of trying to reject efforts even to consider a convention because a convention would be, after all, a countervailing power center to Congress itself. And so, they will be grudging. One of the reasons they have not held hearings on this subject—as Professor Gunther correctly calls on them to do—is that they do not want to make the whole convention process any more credible than it is now. Nonetheless, to say that it is a political question is not to say that there would be no relief if Congress abused its power. My view is that, if there were a sufficient body of applications on a specific subject, or phrased in terms of, "We should like a convention to discuss a balanced budget provision," and if Congress should reject such a valid call, members of Congress would pay a political price over time for that decision, and that is not bad, either.

PROFESSOR BATOR: I agree with the speakers that the central problem will be the validity of the attempt to limit the subject matter of the convention, not whether the calls are contemporaneous. And I agree that these small technical differences among the various resolutions should not become the dominant question. It seems clear that Congress would have to pass a statute calling a convention.

On the central question of validity, I think the issue will be quite sharply focused. If there are thirty-four or more resolutions more or less like the Kansas one, there are two things Congress can do. Congress can take Professor Black's line and say, "You guys have tried to create something that the Constitution does not allow and that would be wholly illegal; therefore, we will do nothing. Take your hats; go home, no convention." That is hospitable to the Kansas resolution if one sees as one of its *central* purposes, the purpose of having no convention unless it is limited to the up-down vote on their specific language. But I do not read the Kansas resolution in that spirit.

The alternative for Congress is to say, "The exact design you have placed before us cannot be accomplished because we all agree that the convention cannot be limited to a yes-no vote on set language." (It would be absurd if the convention were not allowed even to amend the proposed amendment; that would not be a convention.) Then comes the problem for Congress, one that judges face all the time: Do we say that nothing will be done, or do we try to look deeper into the purposes at work and see whether there is a basic purpose that can be accomplished?

I think what Congress ought to say at that point is: "The thirty-four resolutions have in common a specific deep concern about a constitutional shortcoming, and we are obligated and therefore will call a convention to address *that* concern." Article V is clear about one thing: there is an obligation on the part of the Congress that is very explicit; it was not to be discretionary. Congress, therefore, should call a convention for the purpose of addressing the common concern.

Is it sensible to say that these resolutions imply that if we cannot limit the convention to an up-down, yes-no vote on the specific Kansas language, then *nothing* should happen? That seems to me to be not hospitable but the opposite.

PROFESSOR GUNTHER: Unfortunately, though I share Professor Bator's starting point, the text of those resolutions stands in the way of leading the spirit in that direction. He is attributing, I think, to the state legislatures a partly justifiable spirit of making a symbolic gesture of disgust with inflation and deficits and fiscal problems. The fact is, the legislatures were sold this bill of goods by a specific organization that wrote this provision and that does not want the spending proposal but does want the balanced budget proposal. The California legislative resolution on this subject did not pass because, among other reasons, California was the one state in the country that held legislative hearings on the issue. But the legislative counsel of the California Senate and of the California Assembly, who was not at all hostile to Professor Bator's spirit—indeed, favorable to it—said in explaining the California resolution that this provision means that if a convention wants to go ahead and consider the spending amendment, it is going beyond our purpose.

I am not saying that this point totally undercuts Professor Bator's view of reading the spirit of Article V into the state applications. But it is another example of the thoughtlessness behind the process: a particular group sells a particular package to a lot of legislatures that never hold a hearing, never discuss it, and vote, while Congress is silent. And here we sit trying to figure out what the real spirit was. If the real spirit of the resolutions was a spirit of profound ignorance, then we can go beyond that and hope to find a general feeling of disgust about fiscal problems (which, by the way, would bring in abortion as a fiscal issue). But the feeling has been expressed in a devastatingly narrow way.

PROFESSOR BATOR: Just one clarification. Under my reading, the central purpose of the Kansas legislature would be accomplished—the convention would have the opportunity to vote on their specific proposal.

PROFESSOR GUNTHER: What could not be accomplished is Kansas's further purpose that the convention do nothing else if they turn that one particular proposal down.

PROFESSOR BLACK: Everybody has to agree that it emerges plainly from the text of Article V that, if thirty-four valid applications are submitted, then Congress has to call a convention subject to the inevitable condition that is inherent in our system: that members of Congress have to reach agreement and, therefore, can only try to agree. And I hope they would try earnestly to call a convention that they could all agree on as to its call. But this has nothing to do with the question of what is a valid or invalid application, or anything else that we have been talking about, except the truism that an application for a convention for proposing amendments would be valid. And by that, I meant that Congress would have to try to get together and call it.

Now, the problem with this equitable reinterpretation, this doctrine of cy pres and reformation of the state applications, is that it is hard to believe that the states put these limitations in the applications for no reason. And one reason that makes me believe there is a reason is that I have been preaching against such limitations now, for sixteen years, since 1963. Back in those days, they set out the text of an amendment which the convention was to vote up or down. In other words, this is not a practice that is accidental. The attempted limitation of a convention is something that is being tenaciously preserved in the states. Before we leave contract law, let me say that accepting this application and calling a convention which by its nature has to be unlimited is not, it seems to me, an acceptance but a profound distortion of what the Kansas legislature has said they want, as plainly as human language can say it.

PROFESSOR JAMES M. BUCHANAN, Virginia Polytechnic Institute: I would like to correct Professor Gunther on one factual point. Other states besides California have held hearings. I happened to be involved personally in that fiasco with Jerry Brown in New Hampshire. And so, first, I would like to challenge Professor Gunther for treating these state resolutions so peremptorily on the ground that they are ill-thought-out. I do not deny that they are, but surely the Congress is not famous for its wisdom either in many of its considerations. And I do not think there is any difference there between the Congress and the states. If anything, wisdom cuts in favor of the states, I would say.

But the real question I would like to ask of all the participants, with the possible exception of Mr. Silberman, is to think about the underlying political philosophy. I say "think about it" because you will not have time to answer. But think about the political philosophy that is implicit in this discussion. Even Professor Bator—I was going along with him, nodding my head, until he said, "What if there were a libertarian majority?"

The whole philosophy of democracy in America stems from the fact that the people have an opportunity, and if the people want something, that is the way it should happen. The idea that the way the Constitution has developed, the way it has been judicially interpreted, and the way institutions are now set up is somehow sacrosanct—that sort of evolutionist position is one I associate with Michael Oakeshott, and I don't really believe that these distinguished constitutional lawyers would buy Michael Oakeshott for a minute. And yet their position, it seems to me, is to worry excessively about all the uncertainties involved if we turn to a constitutional convention, which is a means created for the people in fact to do something about this mess we are in. Since a convention's work would have to be ratified by three-fourths of the states, I do not see why this concern, this worry about risk and uncertainty, is justified.

PROFESSOR GUNTHER: I would like to go on record in response to Professor Buchanan. It is true of all of us on this panel that we spend a good part of our lives not considering the Constitution sacrosanct and criticizing Supreme Court decisions—disagreeing with some and not others. And we have some claim to belief in the people. But it does seem to me a sloganeering approach to suggest that I am to be judged as being against or for the people if I argue that the people ought to be informed, ought to know what they are doing.

It is true that after the California hearings, there were a couple of hearings elsewhere, including New Hampshire. But it is also true that the twenty-six or twenty-seven states that came aboard before the California hearings very often voted on this without discussion, without awareness of what they were voting for in seeking a convention. I have

35

talked to state legislators and found that, typically, they had *not* thought about this.

Sure, the people are expressing a vague spirit about the budget and the fiscal crisis; *but* they are also invoking Article V of the Constitution. And there is vast confusion, as we are illustrating here, over what that implies. I think it is true respect for the people to say that they ought to know what they are doing when they support a convention—other than making a general gesture which may have consequences many of the people do not intend. And that admonition does not seem to me to be adequately responded to by saying that we are all true-blue defenders of the Constitution as it is written and interpreted, or by arguing about who among us is more on the side of the people.

PROFESSOR BLACK: I am glad the people came into this because I have thought a lot about the people. I have even been reading Sandburg's *Lincoln,* and I want to put my point in two ways. First the counting of state legislatures, one by one, as anybody who opens the *World Almanac* can see, has little to do with understanding democratic expression. Over half the American people now live in nine states of the Union. The ratio between the largest and smallest states is five times as great as it was when the 1787 Constitution went into effect. It is 65 to 1 today, as opposed to about 12 to 1 then.

Second, everybody who tries to get a little mileage out of the people and democracy on this matter should reflect on one fact: There is one institution, only one, in which the American people, the whole American people, are represented pro rata approximately to their population, and that is the national House of Representatives. The state legislatures have the capacity, at least by simply counting them, of very greatly distorting what the majority wants. For example, the three-fourths of the states it takes to ratify a constitutional amendment could be made up of only 40 percent of the American people. Of course, that is not likely to occur, but it does mean that, with the kind of demographic situation we have, it is very possible to get an enormous, overwhelming count of states and still have nothing like the kind of overwhelming consensus of the American people that we would like to have for a constitutional amendment. If you contrast this situation with 1787, you will find that you could not get three-quarters of the states, in any way, without having at least 60 percent of the American people.

MR. SILBERMAN: I should like to defend Professor Bator. I am not sure he will like my defense, but, after all, he did say that implicit in my view—and he is correct—is the assumption that a constitutional convention would turn out to be marginally (and perhaps significantly) more conservative than the present Congress. He was not saying that he was against the democratic will. He was pointing out that the underlying premise of my view necessarily had to be that I thought that the kind of constitutional convention we would have would look hospitably on the proposals and concerns that I described. And that is correct; I do believe that.

To respond to his point that we could end up with little old ladies in tennis shoes on the left dominating a convention, I am not afraid of that because I think there are a lot of reasons why it is unlikely. The most important reason is that in broad, philosophical terms, the left side of our political spectrum already has control of the existing Constitution-amending instrumentalities—the federal judiciary, to a large extent, and the Congress.

But I ask you what political forces would be unleashed if, in fact, there is a call for a constitutional convention to deal with government spending—balanced budget, school prayers, busing, abortion? What kind of political forces will that unleash? What kind of convention will we have? Indeed, the one thing I suspect that Professor Black and I agree on is exactly what kind of a convention we would have.

PROFESSOR BATOR: I would like to return to Professor Buchanan's statement. I have some sympathy for the way he put that statement, because I do think that some of the arguments against the convention are profoundly antidemocratic and reflect unnecessary timidity. I disagree with Professor Black, yet again. In fact, I whispered to Professor Wood that Mr. Black's remarks would have set even Hamilton rolling in his grave. It is Professor Black's opinion that the only legitimate national representative of the people is the Congress; but that is not the Constitution's vision. The Constitution's vision is that the states and the state legislatures represent the people in a different *sense* than the Congress does. What *The Federalist* says about that is that it is not just a matter of voting structure; it is a matter of institutional perspective, it is a matter of how close you live to the people, of what kinds of issues you address, whether they are national or local issues. And I think there is very profound wisdom in the proposition that thirty-four state legislatures speak for the people in a different sense than Congress ever can.

Having said that, let me say where I differ from Professor Buchanan. I do shrink from the idea of an all-purpose, unlimited convention to revise the Constitution, not because I think the existing one is sacrosanct, but because I do not think we have been through the processes of issue framing and debate on fundamentals that are needed to prepare us for that kind of exercise. In fact, I do not even think there

37

is, in the political circumstances of the moment, a great national call for a general revision of the Constitution. What there is is a very serious and profound call for addressing, at the constitutional level, the question of fiscal responsibility and the relationship between expenditures and income. But what strikes me as bizarre is to hear that if we did want a convention to address the question of fiscal responsibility at the constitutional level, the Constitution says that, no matter how much we want it, we cannot have it. And that is what I am hearing from Professor Black.

PROFESSOR WOOD: It seems to me that we cannot see this in any other terms except historical; that is, history impinges on us. We really do not have the alternative of escaping history, and therefore we *are* wrapped up in an evolutionary process. We will make efforts to escape from it, but it is impinging on us.

In historically accurate terms, there was no nation in 1787—no one could have said that the House of Representatives was the only institution that represented the people. Most people thought of the state legislatures as the truly representative institutions. The situation in 1787 was more or less comparable to what is happening in Europe today—they are putting together a European parliament, but most Europeans do not think of that parliament as becoming anything important. It will be the French legislature, the English Parliament, that continue to be important for the foreseeable future. Yet that European supernational parliament may grow into something.

That was the situation in 1787. What we have today is the consequence of two hundred years, and we cannot overturn that. We cannot return to 1787 by some technical provision in the Constitution, which was designed for a different world; there is no way we can do that. This, it seems to me, is the context in which we must look at this issue.

PETER SCHUCK, American Enterprise Institute: Much of the discussion today, particularly Professor Bator's critique of Professor Black, has ignored a few important facts. The first is that there is an alternative mode of constitutional amendment provided for in Article V. It is a procedure whereby the interests of the people, viewed in some abstract sense, as well as the interests of the states would be represented. The Constitution describes certain institutions intended to reflect purely popular sources—that is, the House of Representatives—and others that give certain weight to state interests, such as the Electoral College and the practice at that time of electing United States senators through the state legislatures. So that I do not think it a fair critique of Professor Black's position on Article V to argue that it would deprive the people in the states of a remedy narrowly focused on a particular shortcoming or perceived shortcoming of the Constitution if it were accepted.

It also seems to ignore the fact that the constitutional scheme reflects a concern for the importance of mediating institutions, and conflicts between mediating institutions. It would be a reasonable interpretation of the constitutional convention procedure that the Congress would not merely act as some sort of scribe for the state legislatures, but would exercise an independent judgment, upon the application of those state legislatures, as to what the ground rules and the agenda of that convention would be. The critique that suggests that the people would have no remedy if Professor Black's interpretation were adopted is inaccurate and misses the importance of mediating and conflict between mediating institutions in this process.

PROFESSOR BATOR: Of course, there is a remedy in the sense that one can elect a new Congress which itself might then propose an amendment the states desire. But as one reads the accounts of what led to the compromise of Article V, it was precisely the vision of the framers that there may arise situations in which that would not meet the needs. The great concern that they had centered on intransigence within the central authority; that is why they created this alternative. What I am trying to do is to give a generous reading to the idea that they wanted an *alternative* route for addressing deficiencies in the Constitution.

There was this fear of blockage, and they did not say the way to clear the blockage was to elect a new Congress. You see, they did have very much in mind that even a new Congress may not solve the problem because of the special institutional perspective of becoming a member of the central government. That is a recurring theme in *The Federalist Papers,* that just changing your central governors may not fit the need, may not clear the blockage.

PROFESSOR BLACK: We are back with the people again. It is documented without equivocation in the 1787 debate that those people did not think of the *legislatures* as the *people.* This idea is rebutted by many things, but most of all and most decisively by what was done, and what was said when it was done, in submitting the new Constitution to conventions rather than to the legislatures. They did that, as Madison pointed out in a ringing passage, because they wanted to rest the Constitution on the supreme authority of the *people.*

If a convention is the people, or the only organ of the people that can be assembled, then my view is the one maximally hospitable to change or the proposal of change by the people themselves—much more so than a view that has a convention, the representatives of the people,

39

constrained by some kind of strings or blinders before they can get to work.

The fact is that you could have a petition from forty-one state legislatures for a constitutional convention and still not have a majority of the American people residing in those forty-one states. If we are going to get mileage out of the emotions of democracy, I think we have to ponder facts like that.

JEFFREY T. BERGNER, Office of Senator Richard Lugar: It seems to be the sense of the panel that one cannot formally restrict a constitutional convention to the consideration of a single issue; that, in effect, the entire Constitution would be at risk whenever there is a constitutional convention. Would the panel comment on whether that extends to the ratification requirement in the present Constitution—could a new convention propose a new means of ratification, demanding only twenty-six states, say, or ten? If so, how would that be consistent with any reading of what the framers intended? If not, what is the authorization for exempting this part of the Constitution, that is, for limiting a constitutional convention in this particular way?

MR. SILBERMAN: That is a good question. I think there is a consensus on the panel that it is exceedingly doubtful that anyone, the legislatures or the Congress or a combination of the two, could limit the proposals a convention could make. There are disagreements here as to the validity of state calls that implicitly limit the convention, and there may well be disagreements as to the validity of congressional efforts to limit the agenda. My own view is that the Congress cannot do so.

But if that is so, then the question is, could the constitutional convention abolish a democratic form of government?—which is the logical extension of your question. Well, it could propose anything, but it would still require three-quarters of the state legislatures to ratify.

MR. BERGNER: Could the convention not say that the present ratification requirement did not apply to *its* proposals? And if not, why not? Does not the language of the present Constitution, then, offer a limit to another convention?

MR. SILBERMAN: The convention could not propose a change in the ratification process of its own proposed amendments.

PROFESSOR GUNTHER: Its proposals are not part of the Constitution unless ratified.

PROFESSOR BLACK: I am glad we found a law to agree on up here. The convention could propose an amendment that would in the future change the ratification process, but that amendment would have to pass three-quarters of the states.

PROFESSOR GUNTHER: The only precedent you have for your scenario is the 1787 convention, which did exactly what you suggest.

PROFESSOR WOOD: How is it that the states have been able to have limited conventions?

PROFESSOR GUNTHER: That is a question of their own constitutions. Professor Wood, though I admire you immensely as a historian, I am distressed that you referred to Article V as merely a technical provision of the Constitution. It is *in* this Constitution, with a particular, useful history, cloudy as it may be. The fact that the states have operated differently does not shed much light. The states' actions *have* been talked about, despite your earlier statement—Professor Black has talked about them, the American Bar Association committee has talked about them, and a number of articles have talked about them, mostly concluding that the relevance of the state conventions is not very great. It is *not* that they have been ignored; it is that they have been considered, and considered not terribly helpful.

PROFESSOR WOOD: Why? Why is it not close?

PROFESSOR GUNTHER: On the ground there are different state constitutions, with different histories, with different provisions, and that there is no body of precedent of constitutional law that mingles, as one fungible mass, fifty state constitutions.

PROFESSOR WOOD: But the very idea of a convention came from the state experience in the decade prior to the Constitution.

PROFESSOR BLACK: The pre-1787 experience has been canvassed, and as far as I am aware, there had been no limited state conventions, except ones that had the power to amend without ratification.

PROFESSOR BATOR: I want to come back to the central premise of Professor Gunther's argument. The only thing there seems to be agreement about is that one cannot be *sure* that a convention can be legally and practically limited, but I think that a better case can be made that Congress has power to limit the convention to the issue that evoked the

41

call among the states, and that it is very likely that such a limit can be carried through—that it will be effectuated through the political dynamics—although there is no way of guaranteeing that it will be enforced.

PROFESSOR GUNTHER: I think Congress has the power to state a moral exhortation, but I disagree about the likelihood, in the political dynamics, that that would be a truly effective limitation.

Part Two

The Effects of Constitutional Restraints
on Economic Policy Making

Introduction

Herbert Stein, Chairman

The title of this session is somewhat ambiguous. It could mean, What effects would constitutional restraints have on economic policy making? But it also means, Given constitutional restraints on economic policy making, what effects would that have on the economy or on society at large? We ought to be concerned with both questions.

Also, we are concerned with constitutional restraints that do not now exist, in addition to those that do. A current constitutional restraint on economic policy making is the provision that a person cannot be deprived of property without due process of law, although some people think that that has been contravened, for example, in the price-wage guidelines program. But we are concerned primarily with potential constitutional restraints, provisions that do not now exist.

Since the subject is very broad and we have very able speakers, I will not try to define the discussion more than is implied in the title. I suggest, though, that it would be interesting to learn what the speakers believe the effects of potential constitutional restraints would be on the rate of inflation, on the rate of economic growth, on the quality of the division of the national output between the public and private sectors, among other matters.

Prudent Steps toward a Balanced Budget

Arthur F. Burns

A clear trend has developed in our country in recent years toward ever larger government spending and borrowing. Fifty years ago, in 1929, government expenditure at all levels—federal, state, and local—accounted for approximately 10 percent of the dollar value of our nation's total production of goods and services. The corresponding figure rose to 20 percent in 1940, to 30 percent in 1960, and to 36 percent last year.

These inroads of government into the private sector of our economy reflect, to a large degree, an explosion of federal spending on social programs—income security, education, health, community development, veterans benefits, and so on. The increases in spending have been accompanied by a rapidly rising tax burden. Not only that, our federal government has proved itself incapable of limiting the cost of its programs to the amounts it was prepared to raise in taxes. During the past quarter century, the federal budget has been in balance in only four years, and the size of the deficit has increased enormously during the past decade.

The bias of federal fiscal policy toward larger spending and taxing has reduced incentives of people to work, to save, and to invest. It thus has weakened the vitality of our private economy. Furthermore, persistent federal deficits have become a major driving force of inflation. When our government runs deficits, as it has been doing for many years, it pumps more money into the pocketbooks of people than it takes out of their pocketbooks. That is the way our unprecedented bout with inflation got under way in the mid-1960s, and that is how our inflation has been largely nourished since then.

Inflation in our country has reached dangerous proportions. A few years ago, in 1976, the increase in the consumer price level was a little below 5 percent. The next year, in 1977, it reached 7 percent. Last year, in 1978, it reached 9 percent. This year, as we all know, the inflation rate has been running above 10 percent.

An inflationary psychology is raging in our country. The inflation is being intensified by widespread and growing expectations that rapid inflation will continue. In order to achieve success in the fight against inflation, we will somehow have to find a way of turning inflationary psychology around, so that people will no longer expect rapid inflation to continue indefinitely in the future.

I doubt that such a change in national psychology can be achieved without drastic therapy. A firm requirement for a balanced budget, or some other form of drastic therapy, is now needed to assure the American people that the bias that has emerged in our country toward larger government spending and borrowing is finally being curbed, and that the American public may therefore once again look forward to a dollar of stable purchasing power.

To attain this fundamental objective, I am inclined to recommend that the Congress move toward a constitutional requirement for a balanced budget, but that this be done on a step-by-step basis. I would suggest as the first step a balanced-budget statute rather than a joint congressional resolution calling for a constitutional amendment.

Let me outline, without trying to use legislative language, what the statute that I have in mind might look like. It would begin with a preamble that endorses the principle of a constitutional requirement of a balanced budget and indicates that it is the intent of the Congress to move resolutely in that direction.

The first section of the statute would specify that the planned outlays of the federal government for any fiscal year must not exceed the expected receipts unless our country finds itself in a state of war declared by Congress or unless both houses of Congress decide by something more than a bare majority, let us say by a two-thirds vote, to suspend this budgetary rule.

The purpose of this critical provision of the statute would be to offset our governmental bias toward budget deficits; that is, to reduce the frequency and size of deficits, but not necessarily to eliminate deficits as such. Under this provision the federal government could still deal effectively with military or economic emergencies; it would not be placed in a financial straitjacket. In fact, a deficit of any size could still be voted at any time by the Congress, but the deficit could no longer be achieved by a bare majority of the Congress.

A second section of the statute that I have in mind would deal with the practical problem of unexpected or uncontrollable developments that frequently arise in the fiscal sphere. For example, the economy may fail to generate revenues on the expected scale, or the cost of entitlement programs may exceed estimated magnitudes, or the rate of interest may be higher than expected. This section of the statute would deal with such unexpected fiscal developments in two ways.

The first of these would specify that a small unplanned excess of spending over revenue—up to, let us say, 2 percent of the prescribed expenditure—is to be treated as conforming to the balanced budget requirement. Assume that revenues are estimated at $500 billion, that spending is also estimated at $500 billion, but that spending turns out to be $510 billion. Since the $10 billion excess over the prescribed expenditure comes to only 2 percent, it would be overlooked; that is, the fiscal result would be regarded as conforming to the balanced budget requirement. Obviously, 2 percent is an arbitrary figure; it might be set a little lower or a little higher, but in any case it would need to be small. Otherwise, the intent of the balanced budget principle would be nullified.

But what would happen if the deficit went beyond the 2 percent tolerance? In that event, this section of the statute would specify that the overspending is to be counted as an outlay in the next fiscal year unless a two-thirds majority of each house of the Congress voted either to "forgive" the deficit or to treat all or some part of it as an outlay spread over several of the following years.

To illustrate what I have in mind, let us modify the preceding numerical example. Assume that revenues come up to the expectation of $500 billion, that spending turns out to be $530 billion, and that the tolerable overspending is only $10 billion. Since the overspending turns out to be $30 billion, that amount would be counted as an outlay in the next fiscal year unless both houses of Congress decide by a two-thirds majority either that the overspending is to be forgiven, or that all or some part of the overspent amount is to be treated as an outlay spread over the next three or four years. The purpose of such a statutory provision would be to allow reasonable flexibility in handling any large failures of budgetary estimation that might arise and still protect the budget substantially against the bias of excessive spending and borrowing.

The next section of the statute would seek to limit or restrain the use of fiscal devices that may nullify the spirit of a balanced budget requirement. Many such fiscal devices come readily to mind. To begin with, there is the "off-budget" category of outlays, which came into existence, I believe, in fiscal 1973 with an outlay of under $100 million and that has now grown to something like $12 or $13 billion. That category could easily grow to $20 billion, or to $30 billion, or to a still larger figure if Congress decided to shift some items in the regular budget to the "off-budget" category. Again, Congress could at some future date decide that the balanced budget requirement refers merely to operating expenditures, so that capital outlays are to be excluded. Or to cite another possibility, Congress might decide that federal expenditures on health are to be reduced while employers are being required to establish costly health programs for their workers.

The range of such fiscal devices—whether they are viewed as innovations or circumventions—is endless. This kind of difficulty is inherent, I believe, in all balanced budget proposals. Obviously, a balanced budget requirement is not a panacea. Not only are there means for nullifying its spirit; these means could also involve dubious governmental practices.

I do not think there is any way of completely dealing with this difficulty. Nevertheless, the third section of my suggested statute would deal with it in part by specifying that definitions of key fiscal concepts in existing law or practice—such as budget authority, budget outlay, appropriation, revenue, the public debt, and so on—should be changed only by a two-thirds majority of each house of Congress.

Finally, the fourth section of the statute that I am sketching would provide that appropriate committees of the Congress undertake an annual review, over the next three to five years, of the practical workings and effects of this legislation. A major purpose of the annual reviews would be to determine whether the statute is working out sufficiently well to justify the prospect of moving it, or some suggested modification of it, onto the path of a constitutional amendment. That purpose would need to be spelled out either in the final section of the statute or in the preamble, and the statute itself would be limited to three or five years.

The course of action that I am suggesting for dealing with the budget is, I think, a prudent course. It involves a step-by-step approach. It argues, in effect, that just as a troublesome bias in our nation's fiscal policies has been demonstrated by experience, so we should also be guided by accumulated experience as we work toward the objective of a constitutional remedy.

If the statute that I sketched were adopted this year, it might go far in subduing the inflationary expectations that are plaguing our economy. Indeed, such a statute might accomplish more in this direction than would an immediate congressional call for a constitutional amendment. The latter course would inevitably involve our fifty states in prolonged debate and might not reach a positive result even after several years have elapsed.

Let me close by saying that in my judgment the sort of statute that I have proposed would not only help to curb inflationary expectations. It would also help to restore confidence, now badly shaken, in our nation's government and in the integrity of our nation's currency.

Balancing the Budget versus Limiting Spending

Wm. Craig Stubblebine

Constitutional limits on federal tax, spending, and budget powers, desirable or not, do exist. For those who have not seen it, I would call attention to Kenneth Dam's "The American Fiscal Constitution" in the *University of Chicago Law Review,* winter 1977, which presents a well-developed case for the existence of a fiscal constitution. One might take exception to some of the provisions he identifies, particularly those that he labels "constitutional" with a small *c*, but he does present a compelling case. The central concern, therefore, is not whether we should have such limits, but whether the provisions now extant in the Constitution will be modified by new language.

It seems to me the current options are to do nothing, to pursue some sort of balanced budget amendment, to pursue a spending limit amendment, to pursue a tax limitation amendment, or to pursue some other amendment whose outlines are not yet clear. Simply that the alternatives are being discussed, that this conference is being held, reflects a significant dissatisfaction on the part of the American body politic with the performance of the government, whether that dissatisfaction is rightly or wrongly placed.

First the facts: There has been an increasing intrusion of government into the life of our nation, in the form of taxes, spending, and regulation. Not the least of these intrusions is the current handling of the oil market. I cannot resist the temptation to suggest that if we tried to handle other commodity markets—corn, beef, wheat, and so forth— the way we are trying to handle oil, we would have shortages everywhere. The fact is that government no longer is merely a background within which people organize their daily lives. It is no longer confined to establishing and enforcing property rights and providing for the national defense. It is now an active participant in the life of the nation— in the energy crisis, in personal investment decisions influenced by their tax consequences, and on and on.

The second fact is inflation. I am not going to detail the intrusions that fuel inflation. Everybody knows about them. The issue is the performance of the government as reflected in this fact. I am not suggesting that there is unanimity that the performance is bad or defective; I am suggesting only that a significant portion of the body politic is dissatisfied.

What are the causes of these two facts? That is, why do we have this increasing intrusion; why do we have inflation?

The first answer is that an increasingly sophisticated economy presents increased opportunities for government intervention. It may also present demands for intervention, but at the very least it does present the opportunities. Many regulations that now exist would simply be unenforceable in a less well-developed, less sophisticated economy. The notion of income and its direct taxation, for instance, can only be found, really, in a sophisticated, developed economy. It is no accident that the Sixteenth Amendment was not passed until 1913, until the economy reached that degree of sophistication. William H. Riker gets at this in his paper "The Cause of Public Sector Growth." I cite that paper because his conclusions and mine coincide at least at that point.

The second cause of the two facts is the coalition process in government. For each one of us, government spending on a program offers the least-cost way of providing that service. Classic examples, of course, are programs whose benefits accrue to a narrow group of people, but which are funded by general taxation. The tax price of the marginal cost to the individual beneficiaries appears to be zero. That they should demand unlimited numbers of those programs, each of unlimited size, should come as no surprise. And this is true of all of us. We are all beneficiaries of some program, and so increased spending has its proponents. At the same time, taxes are painful and we prefer lower total taxes.

The conjunction of these two factors—opportunity to intervene and support for this or that intervention—leads to budget deficits, which lead in turn to money creation and finally to inflation. The coalition process also leads to government regulation—in fact, given these causes, the phenomenon that really needs to be explained is why government does not regulate 100 percent of the economy. Admittedly, these causes are speculative, and the theoretical modeling remains to be done. I suggest them, though, because other explanations are difficult or opaque or have contradictory phenomena.

What we have now are the issue, the facts, and the cause. What we need is the cure. The first option, of course, is to do nothing, to conduct business as usual. The second do-nothing alternative is to try to elect a different group of representatives. The third kind of do-nothing alternative is to enact new legislation, such as Kemp-Roth indexing or any of a whole host of measures that have been introduced into Congress.

Business-as-usual is an appropriate strategy if, and only if, Congress believes that nothing more deleterious will happen, such as, for example, a balanced budget constitutional convention. Electing a different group of representatives is not likely to change the basic situation, given the causes enunciated above. New representatives will merely replace old representatives in the same old institutional decision-making setting. They will find the pressures to increase spending and cut taxes to be as real as those that beset their predecessors.

As far as new legislation is concerned, one Congress cannot bind future Congresses. A simple majority of both houses and the president can repeal any statute. Legislation also suffers from another defect, in my opinion: legislation of the sort necessary will force hard choices and thus will create the very circumstances that are likely to give rise to the required majorities for amending or repealing it. This is to say that when such legislation becomes binding, the Congress then in session may well want to avoid the hard choices that it presents.

If we choose not to do nothing, then we have the balanced budget alternative, a version of which Dr. Burns has outlined just now. Another version is the NTLC-Heinz-Stone amendment, which limits spending, or at least ties increases in federal outlays to increases in GNP. Tax limitations are something else.

Regarding tax limitations, I cannot resist quoting a comment by a student who was examining Proposition 13 in a paper for Peter Drucker. He said:

> One of the clearest admissions that we do not know how to cut government is the implied theory of government embodied in Proposition 13, and its progeny. It can best be summarized by Howard Jarvis's epithet, "The bastards can't spend what they don't have." Neanderthal in its sophistication, merciless in its application, the strategy is simply to limit revenues to a point that the electorate deems appropriate and then let the government officials work it out from there. The fact that this might be the only thing that works is a sobering thought.

Tax limitations aside, what would be the consequences for economic policy making of either a balanced budget constraint or a spending limit constraint contained in a constitutional amendment? I grant that these options have many subsidiary issues in common, but it seems to me necessary to examine them separately because they have different focal points or cutting edges. A balanced budget amendment focuses on balancing the budget, that is, bringing something called revenues into equality with something called outlays or expenditures. Such an amendment directly addresses neither the levels of taxing and spending nor inflation. A spending limit focuses on limiting spending, that is keeping something called outlays or expenditures at or below some predetermined level. Such an amendment directly addresses neither taxation (and hence a balanced budget) nor inflation. For purposes of discussion, let us assume that Congress and the administration seek to live within the spirit of the respective amendments with no subterfuge, no violation, no twisting of the boundaries.

A balanced budget amendment would seek to achieve its balance by either decreasing spending or increasing taxes or some combination of these. Given the current mood of the body politic, it seems to me likely that Congress would tend more toward spending cuts than toward tax increases. As a result, the initial implementation of a balanced budget amendment is likely to be compatible with a spending limit. However, once this mood subsides, coalition politics can be expected to move spending ahead, though at a somewhat slower pace than would occur without a balanced budget amendment. A balanced budget requirement in a recession period demands a fiscal policy of cutting both taxing and spending—or increasing both. It leaves the Federal Reserve with the power to increase the money supply, though without the ready mechanism of a budget deficit. Diminished emphasis on new spending programs can reduce the pressure on the Federal Reserve to inflate the money supply, especially during inflation or stagflation, but the board may still be tempted at such times to opt for an inflationary policy— that is, to avoid the political consequences of so-called exorbitant interest rates and recession.

A spending limit, for the most part, would cause no long-term problems. At worst—or at best, depending on one's point of view—it would keep the share of GNP that government spends where it is at ratification. It would prevent undertaking new programs that necessitate an increase in the share of GNP. During fiscally conservative periods a spending limit would facilitate decreasing the share of GNP used for government expenditures. During fiscally liberal periods, when there was a broad consensus in the body politic, the limitation would permit an increase in the share of GNP used.

The challenging provision in the NTLC-Heinz-Stone amendment is the inflation penalty, particularly as it operates in conjunction with the lag to base. If inflation, as measured, exceeds 3 percent, federal spending declines both as a share of GNP and in real terms. Under that condition, coalition politics would suffer a dual penalty. On the one hand, it takes the heat for the inflation, and, at the same time, it is unable to satisfy the real spending interest of coalition members.

In consequence, Congress would have an incentive to control inflation, or at least to keep it below 3 percent. That is, the amendment would give Congress an incentive to adopt a set of policies that would bring about relatively stable prices. One might speculate what this set of policies would be, but it does seem to me likely that it would include a significant decrease in the pattern of budget deficits. And hence, the spending limitation amendment would be compatible with a balanced budget.

As far as we can tell, a spending limit would have a countercyclical effect, encouraging spending to decline relatively as the economy moves ahead and increase relatively as the economy lags behind. There is an issue here, I think, whether the incentives are strong enough. But merely imposing the penalty—merely cutting or holding down federal spending—would itself tend to diminish deficits and may in fact foster different attitudes toward Federal Reserve policy, particularly interest rates. Indeed, it may even lead to some tolerance of recession on the part of Congress.

I hope this discussion has made clear the essential difference between a balanced budget amendment and a spending limit amendment. The spending limit amendment addresses the level of spending but does not prejudge the appropriateness of particular anti-inflation price policies. It leaves that matter entirely up to Congress to experiment with and sort out.

Also, the spending limit ends the positive payoff that Congress now derives from inflation, whereas the balanced budget amendment does nothing to end this payoff. And we have to keep in mind that the progressive income tax in conjunction with inflation, in the present context, gives Congress the best of all possible worlds. It can both increase tax revenues and cut tax rates at the same time. So it can appear to be sensitive to the body politic while in fact subverting its interests.

What if Congress and the administration resist the spirit of the amendments or seek to subvert them? They could do this by manipulating the definitions of revenues, expenditures, the budget, nominal GNP, real GNP, outlays, nonbudget, off-budget, and on-budget items, non-Treasury spending authority, and so forth. Also, the government could subvert an amendment by seeking to accomplish through regulatory activities the same policy it would otherwise, in the absence of the amendment, pursue through a spending program. Or, it may undertake a new tax expenditure policy, adjusting tax credits and deductions to accomplish its ends. It might seek to manipulate the budget and spending mix to induce popular demand either for an increase in the spending limit or for repeal of a balanced budget amendment or a spending limit amendment.

It is on this point that Robert Bork is concerned that defense will be sacrificed. At the same time, liberals worry that social welfare programs will be sacrificed to defense. It is an interesting anomaly that both Bork and the liberals are concerned about the operation of the amendment, even though their interests are directly contrary. At issue, of course, is the behavior of politicians and bureaucrats as they attempt to live within the Constitution.

My personal concern here involves the so-called emergency clauses. Both the balanced budget and the spending limit proposals have emergency provisions that permit overriding their specifications during an emergency, whatever that means, if approved by extraordinary majorities. An emergency clause seems to me to be a virtual invitation to do business on an emergency basis, to have "government by emergency." It may have the effect simply of increasing the size of the working coalition within which Congress has to operate. I wish I knew what effects that would have on the level or pattern of spending, but, at least to my knowledge, no one has yet developed the theoretical models that might disclose those effects.

I suggest strongly that the courts cannot be expected to police Congress with respect to an emergency clause. That is, the courts cannot be expected to decide when an economic situation justifies an imbalance in the budget or emergency spending above a preset limit. This is an inherent weakness, but I know of no way to avoid it.

We might also face the issue of inept management of the limit. How does one police it? What happens if the government overspends inadvertently? Dr. Burns has indicated one set of penalties if revenues and expenditures do not coincide, and there are some others in the context of a spending limit.

Let me spend just a moment on a comment specific to the NTLC-Heinz-Stone amendment. The original NTLC version had a provision for increasing the spending limit if approved by a three-fourths vote of Congress and ratified by a majority of the state legislatures. In the current NTLC-Heinz-Stone amendment, however, it would require only three-fourths of the Congress. It seems to me that dropping the provision for ratification by the state legislatures does Congress a disservice. Without this, the amendment is prey to the same dangers as any emergency provision: its effect may simply be to increase the size of the working coalition. This *may* retard the growth of government spending or the growth of intervention in the economy, but it may not.

The case of California may be suggestive here. That state has had for many years a constitutional requirement of two-thirds to adopt the annual budget, but this seems not to have had much effect on increases in spending in the California context. There is nothing about extraordinary majorities that suggests they control spending. One might argue, of course, that California's spending would have been significantly higher had the budgets operated by simple majorities. I suppose the ultimate answer here is some form of national referendum, but I, at least, was prepared to live with the provision for ratification by the state legislatures.

Some may be troubled by the question, What if Congress cannot find a set of policies to control inflation? I, personally, am not worried about this because it seems to me that the operation of the limit would then tend automatically to produce budget surpluses, which in themselves should have an anti-inflationary impact.

I would be the last to suggest that this is the ultimate amendment. We would have to see how things go under the amendment to know what kinds of intolerance or what kinds of subversion might greet it and what kinds of weakness of spirit Congress might evidence. I can certainly foresee a new amendment dealing with regulatory activities of the Congress, and we might have to do something later about emergencies or about a national referendum. The important point here is that the spending limit amendment would be compatible with any new amendment that I at least could foresee.

Discretionary Control
of the Federal Budget

James T. McIntyre, Jr.

Analogies never seem quite to illustrate the point they are intended to make, but I want to use one anyhow. It might help put some aspects of the balanced budget debate in proper perspective.

A new recruit in the paratroops was progressing very nicely through basic training until the time came for his first jump. He was just plain scared. His sergeant had to work very hard to calm the young man's fears. He explained that the jump was very simple: the recruit had merely to jump, count to ten, and pull the rip cord. In the unlikely event that the chute did not open, the recruit should count to five and then pull the emergency cord. That would certainly release the chute.

Then the sergeant explained that when the recruit landed, he should detach and fold the chute and walk to the edge of the field, where a bus would be waiting to take him and his buddies to the enlisted men's club. There they would have a big beer bust to celebrate their first jump.

The recruit finally got up the courage to jump. He counted to ten and pulled the rip cord. The chute did not open. He counted to five and pulled the emergency cord. The chute still did not open. As the recruit dropped through space past some of his buddies, who were floating safely to earth, he yelled, "I'll bet you a pitcher of beer that that damned bus ain't waitin' at the edge of the field, either."

I worry that a balanced budget amendment would put the nation's economy in the place of that recruit. The economy would not have a soft landing either.

At the outset, I would like to state as simply and as clearly as possible the administration's position in the balanced budget debate. First, the president has said many times that he is firmly committed to balancing the budget, and the administration is moving the budget rapidly toward balance. Second, the administration believes that a constitutional amendment or legislation containing an unyielding requirement that the budget be balanced except during periods of war and national emergencies is neither feasible nor in the nation's best interest.

Our basic premises are that the government exists to promote the general welfare and that what best promotes the general welfare changes

57

with changing circumstances. Our Constitution establishes a general framework within which the government must operate and enunciates the fundamental principles under which we are to live. More specific rules, or laws, which change with changing conditions, are enacted by the Congress to carry out the general mandate. Many of these rules, or laws, recognize the reality that what is in the nation's best interest changes over time, and they leave to the president some discretion about what to recommend. The laws governing the budget are of this nature.

The Budget and Accounting Act requires that the president transmit to the Congress a budget, but says that the budget shall contain:

> estimated expenditures and proposed appropriations necessary *in his judgment* for the support of the Government for the ensuing year. . .;

> estimated receipts of the Government during the ensuing fiscal year, under (1) laws existing at the time the Budget is transmitted and also (2) *under the proposals*, if any, contained in the Budget." [Emphasis added.]

Then, of course, the Congress exercises its judgment on the president's recommendations. We believe that this provision for the exercise of judgment—rather than a rigid requirement that the budget be balanced—was proper when the act was passed in 1921; we believe that it is still proper.

The desirability of a balanced budget, a surplus, or a deficit at any particular time depends upon which budget best serves the nation's interest. Making this decision is the very heart of the political process. Let me cite three examples of such general policy issues from the history of the last two decades.

The first example concerns the period from roughly 1958 to 1964. During this time the economy was blessed with a relatively low rate of inflation, but it was burdened with a general tendency toward high unemployment. Two recessions and sluggish growth were major issues of this period. In 1962–1964, the administration adopted a fiscal policy of tax reductions. The economy experienced mild deficits, very modest rates of inflation, strong investment and income growth, and declining unemployment rates.

In contrast, in the late 1960s the government attempted simultaneously to increase federal spending for domestic programs and a foreign war and to avoid tax increases. The result of these incompatible objectives was a $25 billion deficit in a year when the economy was fully employed. This set off an inflationary spiral that is still going on. Most of the proposals for requiring annually balanced budgets provide for exceptions in case of war or national emergency. Given the congressional support for the policies that I have just mentioned, plus Congress's specific exemption of Vietnam spending from outlay limitations enacted in 1968, it is likely that the $25 billion deficit and resulting inflation would have occurred even had we had a balanced budget amendment.

The third case occurred in the mid-1970s, when the Ford administration was wrestling with double-digit inflation even before the start of the oil crisis. The oil crisis resulted in massive price increases and simultaneously helped push the U.S. economy into a recession. In addition, droughts in major agricultural areas caused crop shortages and sharply higher prices for farm products. The government could have reacted mechanically, raising taxes and reducing spending in an effort to stem inflation. Clearly, such an approach would have had some moderating influence on price increases—if you make people poor enough, they will not bid prices up. But that approach would have had a devastating effect on the economy. One recent study indicates that a balanced budget strategy would have produced an unemployment rate above 11 percent for two years. Both the Ford and Carter administrations have recognized that pursuit of a balanced budget in those circumstances would have had disastrous effects on incomes and employment.

These three different policies each arose in response to unique circumstances. No single long-term constitutional requirement would have been appropriate for these varying circumstances. The one policy among them that was clearly inflationary and mistaken could have occurred in spite of a balanced budget amendment, whereas the two that were relatively successful would have been prohibited under such an amendment.

The administration believes for several reasons that a constitutional amendment requiring that the budget be balanced is not in the nation's best interest. The federal government cannot ignore the economic force it exerts in our economy and the world economy. Moreover, the government cannot avoid the responsibility it has to make that force a positive one or, at least, not a negative one. This is not to say that the federal government can "fine-tune" the economy. We cannot. But we must at least refrain from reinforcing major adverse swings in the economy.

In this sense, the federal government is different from state and local governments. In a highly integrated national economy, not even a Proposition 13 exerts a major economic impact on the entire nation. This gives state and local governments a degree of fiscal freedom that the federal government does not enjoy. We are synonymous with the economy and are held responsible for its condition. They are not.

A balanced budget amendment would prevent the federal budget from being a discretionary instrument of economic policy. Apparently, its advocates believe that Congress and the president cannot be trusted to manage economic affairs intelligently. Or else they believe that the economic affairs of the nation do not need to be managed. Let me suggest a few of the implications of this position.

First, it would imbed in the Constitution myopic fiscal policy. The federal budget now contains certain automatic stabilizers that have served us well in the postwar period. When the economy is strong, rising tax receipts and lower transfer payments diminish budgetary stimulus. When the economy is weak, these effects are reversed, lending budgetary support to the economy.

Under the balanced budget requirement—and under at least some of the spending limitation proposals—this stabilization would be lost. A recession, which produces lower receipts, would require tax increases and spending cuts—actions that would deepen the recession. And, conceivably, an inflationary boom which balanced the budget would simply provide room for further budgetary stimulus.

Second, the position of the advocates of a balanced budget amendment appears to be that Congress and the president can be trusted with affairs such as the national defense—but not with measures to promote national prosperity. Most proposed balanced budget amendments show recognition that in times of war or national emergency the limit should not be binding. Would Congress not be forced by circumstances to discover emergencies or budgetary gimmicks to escape the controls, for example, when unemployment is rising?

The balanced budget amendment would thus be an open invitation to "creative budgeting" and accounting. Unless the Constitution not only mandates a balanced budget but also clearly and specifically spells out the accounting principles underlying the budget, it would be possible to design all sorts of escape mechanisms. Such escape mechanisms may lead to more costs—financial and economic—and could result in misleading the public and even the budget makers themselves. If the president and the Congress cannot resist political pressures to control spending—as proponents of a balanced budget amendment contend—they certainly cannot be expected to resist such pressures in order to adhere to arbitrary rules of budgeting.

Third, a balanced budget amendment to the Constitution could put the judiciary in ultimate charge of the budget. Were the amendment enacted, the judicial branch would be required to police the president and Congress to make certain they conformed to the amendment. It is not hard to imagine circumstances where the judiciary would be called upon to establish budget concepts in order to police the amendment. This, I submit, would make a farce of the budget process.

Some persons who favor budget restraint recognize the shortcomings of a balanced budget amendment and would impose a different kind of restraint. One such group would restrict federal spending to a certain stipulated percentage of the economy, as measured by GNP.

The problems that exist with respect to this approach are nearly as difficult as those of the balanced budget requirements. For example, if a constitutional amendment or a law were adopted with a spending limit requirement, can we change the definition of GNP? Shall we now include unmarketed housewives' services or illicit drug traffic to "reduce" the federal role in the economy? Shall the courts rule on how GNP and its components are measured?

Alternatively, if Congress, in its wisdom, chose to make large-scale expenditures under the guise of tax subsidies, who would prohibit it? Or suppose that, instead of setting up a federal tax or spending program to promote employment, which would be recorded in the budget, Congress adopted a regulatory approach to require that private businesses increase employment. Would that be unconstitutional or illegal? There are, as we have learned painfully, almost always regulatory—and inflationary—equivalents for budget policies. The practical difficulties of many of these spending limitation proposals are immense.

Even assuming that a balanced budget amendment or legislation were adopted, it would not be enforceable. The relationship between the budget and the economy does not go only from the budget to the economy. It works in both directions.

When the economy slows down, federal receipts fall and some spending (for example, for unemployment benefits) increases. Budget surpluses fall or deficits increase automatically. The historical record on this is very clear. For instance, look at what happened to the federal budget as a result of the economic crises of 1837, 1893, and 1929, not to mention the recent severe recession. In situations like these, trying to balance the budget is like King Canute's trying to hold back the sea by speaking sharply to it. It would be folly to attempt it.

We have an effective mechanism for dealing with the issue of the balanced budget. It is called the budget process. Especially since 1974, when the Congressional Budget Act established systematic procedures for Congress to review the budget, a mechanism has been in place for open and thorough congressional consideration of whether a balanced budget should be adopted. A recent amendment to the debt ceiling law made consideration by both the president and Congress of a balanced budget an explicit requirement, and it did so in a way that would ensure full debate of the issue. A constitutional amendment or legislation to require a balanced budget would presumably shut off such debate. It would make a mockery of the democratic process by denying Congress the power to act on fiscal matters that are profoundly important to the welfare of its constituents.

The essence of the budgetary art is to manage resources prudently in the national interest. The administration remains committed to such prudent management in the context of a sound economy and an effective federal program. Both the president's budget and the totals emerging from Congress this year point toward an orderly transition to a balanced budget. In addition, both the executive branch and Congress are making substantial progress toward multiyear budgeting and planning.

This progress is essential to the realization of effective fiscal restraint. There is now a popular consensus for this objective. With presidential support and congressional efforts at budget restraint, I have little doubt that continuing progress will be made. I am particularly pleased with the technical progress that both the executive branch and Congress have made in carrying out the budget review and planning process. With multiyear planning and zero-based budgeting, we have developed far more effective tools to control the budget. These are the right tools—the only responsible tools—to use for balancing the budget. We intend to use them vigorously.

Constitutional versus Discretionary Constraints

Bruce K. MacLaury

The Gallup poll indicated a year ago that about 80 percent of the populace favored a balanced budget amendment to the Constitution. And, at the last count I saw, thirty of the thirty-four states necessary had passed some form of resolution calling upon Congress to establish a constitutional convention to consider a balanced budget amendment. Moreover, this session of Congress has seen a flowering of resolutions and bills designed to increase fiscal responsibility at the federal level.

Previous speakers have outlined the reasons for this, and each of us has his own checklist. It clearly has to do—as Dr. Burns said at the outset—with a feeling toward big government, toward the fact that federal social programs, and transfer payments in particular, have been growing rapidly while at the same time we see and we read about inefficiency and waste in these programs and in the federal government—in Medicaid programs, CETA programs, GSA, and so on. We find ourselves increasingly tied up and inhibited by regulation and red tape; and probably most of all, we feel ourselves caught in the vise of inflation in this country.

It was Arthur Okun who said that for perhaps the first time in our society, the corrosive effects of inflation, at work now for a number of years, have made everybody feel he is getting the short end of the stick. That is true, and it is why we are thrashing about, if I may put it that way, looking for remedies to the disease of inflation, even through constitutional reform.

Professor Stubblebine said that there are already limits within the Constitution. Mr. McIntyre referred to the limits on spending established by the 1974 Congressional Budget Act. We do have limits, but clearly, they have not worked in a way to prevent the feeling of unease that verges almost on crisis.

Dr. Burns just used the phrase "drastic therapy"—drastic therapy that is needed to change inflation psychology, inflationary expectations. But out of that feeling of crisis have come what I would describe as remedies that in their most blatant form—and by that I *do* mean a constitutional amendment for a balanced budget—are even worse than

63

the disease from which we suffer, bad as that is. In light of the facts and the interpretations of them that the speakers have presented, we have to ask just what is it that these proposals, born out of frustration, would actually remedy.

First, neither of the constitutional amendments for spending limits or for balanced budgets—and it is imperative to keep those two distinct—would do anything *directly* to curb inefficiency and waste in governmental operations. Indirectly, they might add pressures to reduce spending, but we would still read of fraud.

Second, they would do nothing in and of themselves to curb the regulatory excesses that we see every day. And yet, it seems to me that regulatory excesses are as much a cause of the frustration we feel as anything else.

Third, neither of the proposed amendments would do anything about the myriad microdecisions at the federal level on existing programs. In the mid-1960s, the basic fiscal problem leading to inflation was excessive deficits. But in recent years, these microdecisions have done more to increase inflation than our admittedly very large deficits. In citing microdecisions, I am referring to the increase in payroll taxes for social security, to the increases in minimum wages that were voted despite substantial opposition. I am referring to acreage allotments and to crop price-support decisions; to import limitations and "trigger prices" for steel; referring indeed to the whole raft of regulatory decisions which have added substantial costs—call them burdens—to the private sector of the economy.

In each of these areas—waste, regulation, and price-raising microdecisions—the problems from which we are suffering would not be remedied by constitutional amendment. That does not mean that amendments would not have an impact, of course. But I agree with Dr. Burns that four surpluses in the last twenty-five years is a record that no economist of sound mind would try to defend and that biases in our political system tend to engender more spending and more deficits than a responsible policy would call for.

None of today's speakers is saying that there can never be deficits. What we are looking for is a way to change the weight of evidence, that is, to change the presumption as to what can lead to and justify deficits or increasing expenditures.

I happen to believe that we already have an appropriate tool in the congressional budget process as it has evolved in the last few years. This is a tool that has been honed by Congress itself, though admittedly thrust upon it when it began. The process needs further amendment and strengthening in directions that a number of people have pointed out. Mr. McIntyre, just now, referred to the thrust toward improvement coming out of the last debt ceiling legislation, which requires for the first time an explicit look at how budgets will be balanced. The wording of the Senate's first budget resolution this past spring contained the requirement that Congress set second- and third-year targets, in addition to current-year goals. Moreover, in the second resolution, actual guidelines for spending and taxing will be established, which must be followed unless committees can convince the full Congress that a departure is justified.

In the context of blockbuster proposals like the constitutional amendments, it is a modest proposal that Congress be required to set targets for three years ahead, and then be required to abide by them or to justify not abiding by them. But this modest change could tip the scales toward greater fiscal responsibility, without putting so much weight on the scales as to unbalance the whole economy.

Dr. Burns and others have identified one of the real problems with these balanced budget amendments: the problem of defining budget terms. There are a myriad of ways to get around a balanced "budget" requirement. It is an innovative idea in the third section of Dr. Burns's hypothetical bill that definitions must somehow be set forth. But it seems to me that human ingenuity is not likely to be bound by definitions written into the law.

I would like to see how Dr. Burns would respond to a challenge. I admired him during the many years he and I worked together at the Federal Reserve—and I admire him now—but I recall that when Congress tried to bind the Federal Reserve to particular money growth rate targets, it was Dr. Burns who was looking for leeway, for discretionary monetary policy. And now there is the same sort of effort to bind the hands of Congress by means of a balanced budget amendment. It seems strange to me to hear constraints advocated by someone who looked for ways of making more flexible the constraints that were being imposed upon us at the Federal Reserve.

Discussion

PROFESSOR STEIN: I am not a fan of constitutional amendments on budgetary policy. There is no current provision in the Constitution whose validity is so conditional; that is, when we abolished slavery or gave women the vote in the Constitution, we did not say, let's try this for a while and see how it works. But the validity of the budget amendments is very much conditioned upon transitory economic circumstances and on a set of national values that may also be changing. I can give a great deal of support to the statute part of Dr. Burns's proposal, but very little support to the constitutional amendment part. That is, I feel some confidence in prescribing budget policy for the next three or five or seven years, but very little confidence in prescribing it for the next thirty or fifty or seventy years.

This is partly because I have a somewhat different view from some others here of what the consequences of deficits or surpluses might be. Specifically, I do not think that inflation is the inevitable consequence of deficits. I think we could go on with very large deficits for a very long time without inflation. I do think that excessive deficits at the wrong time, and especially excessive increases in deficits, have an inflationary impact, but even that is not insuperable. The major persistent consequence of deficits is that they absorb funds that would otherwise be available for private investment and thereby reduce the rate of economic growth. And it seems to me that the value of economic growth is a subject on which society ought to be able to make a choice from time to time. The case for a high rate of growth is very strong today, but this may not always be true.

An essential aspect of the budget proposition is the way it has been laid out: that we have a choice between one of these amendments and doing nothing. But isn't it a little quick to rule out the possibility of improving the budgetary process by means short of an amendment? I think it is even a little quick to deny the possible value of the Congressional Budget Act, which is, after all, not very old.

In fact, our whole wave of concern about this matter, our view of it as a great national problem, is not very old. Ten years ago, perhaps, we were all fairly satisfied with the performance of budget policy in the preceding half-century or more; we did not see anything terribly wrong with it. So I do not think we now have evidence of a great, built-in, persistent bias in the system that can only be corrected by a radical transformation, as a constitutional amendment would be. I still have some hope that we can learn more about how to manage budget policy. Besides, I don't think the amendments would relieve us of the necessity for learning because, even with the balanced budget amendment, the question whether this is the time for a surplus or the time for a deficit would always be present.

What I fear as the consequence of the current discussion is that it might short-cut the whole process of trying to learn what fiscal policy ought to be like and trying to educate the public about what it ought to be like, and might substitute for that process of learning and education acquiescence in an existing popular prejudice. And while I recognize the legitimacy of paying attention to that popular prejudice, still, when I think of a lot of other popular prejudices—such as what profits the oil companies ought to make, or whether we should have price and wage controls, and a lot of other things—I do not feel entirely committed to living with things that will be supported by an 80 percent vote in the Gallup polls. So I am cool to the amendment propositions.

Would any of the panel members like to respond?

DR. BURNS: I don't know that I would like to respond, but I deem it a duty to respond.

Mr. MacLaury put a question to me. He pointed out quite correctly the stand that I took with regard to congressional insistence at one time that the Federal Reserve System operate on the basis of mechanical rules with regard to the money supply and the like. I objected at the time, and I would object again today.

The question put to me is how do I reconcile the position that I took with regard to congressional mandates concerning monetary policy and the view that I have expressed today about fiscal policy.

First of all, let me say that if my friend Bruce MacLaury or anyone else thinks that I'm being inconsistent, that is the least of my worries. I've lived a long life. I've had to learn and relearn my economics time and again, and I'm still in the process of trying to do that.

But let me give a more serious answer. Bruce referred to a term that I used, "drastic therapy." I used that term deliberately. As I see things, our country is now involved in an inflationary spiral that is being fed by an inflationary psychology.

Businessmen are willing to grant sizable—sometimes even outrageous—wage increases because they feel they can pass them on to the consuming or business public in the form of higher prices. Workmen and their trade unions insist on large nominal wage increases in part because of the inflation that has taken place, and in part because of the increase in the consumer price level that they expect will take place in the future. Bankers insist on what are historically very high interest rates—at least in part because they expect to be paid back in cheaper dollars. Businessmen and consumers are willing to pay these high interest rates, partly because many feel that a house or a machine bought today is acquired at a bargain price when compared with the price that will have to be paid next month or next year. And, I need hardly add, borrowers also feel that they can repay their loans in cheaper dollars.

This inflationary psychology is dangerous. It means that people have come to feel that money is a depreciating asset while commodities are appreciating assets. I don't think that we can bring inflation under control unless or until the current inflationary psychology is changed.

I read in the newspapers about debates in the Congress. One question concerns the federal budget deficit for fiscal 1980. Should it be $29 billion, as the president originally recommended, or maybe only $20 billion or $23 billion? There are also debates between members of the administration and officials of the Federal Reserve, sometimes even public debates, about the appropriate level of the federal funds rate— the one interest rate that the Federal Reserve System controls rather directly. The debate here centers on the question whether the federal funds rate should be 10 percent or perhaps 10¼ or 10½ percent.

These are interesting debates. They indicate something about the direction of economic policy that this or that individual or group believes is desirable. But to my way of thinking, the world will be much the same whether the current debate on fiscal policy is resolved one way or the other. I feel likewise with regard to current debates on monetary policy.

Marginal adjustments around which so much of our debating centers will make little difference in the actual world. To change inflationary psychology much more is required; something needs to be done that will be regarded as truly significant by the general public with regard to the environment in which they function.

Working toward a constitutional requirement for a balanced budget, an idea that I've approached cautiously, may well produce the kind of change in inflationary psychology that I think is now required to bring inflation under some control. I can think of other forms of drastic therapy. I didn't mention them, and I don't intend to do that now; we've got enough of a problem today in dealing with fiscal matters.

Now, let me turn more directly to Mr. MacLaury's question. The debates that I had with members of the Congress related to mechanical monetary rules and I was opposed to them. The kind of fiscal plan that I talked about today has essential elements of flexibility. It is not a mechanical plan. It does not call for a balanced budget, year in and year out. The logic underlying it is very simple: since a bias toward deficits has governed our fiscal policy in recent decades, it is important to our nation's future to limit or to offset that bias. The proposal that I've made attempts to do that without putting the Congress in a straitjacket.

Whether or not there is any sympathy for my plan, I hope that everyone will at least recognize the bias in our fiscal policies and ponder ways of correcting it.

Finally, let me say this: Those of us who are fighting for some kind of drastic therapy for dealing with inflation seem to be having an influence that deserves to be noted. I listened with great interest to the conservative fiscal views expressed by my erstwhile colleague, Bruce MacLaury—I expected that from him. I was similarly impressed by what my more recent colleague, Jim McIntyre, had to say. I knew that those were his personal views, but he spoke today for the administration and that is important. He expressed sound, conservative views, speaking for the administration. I'm not sure he would have expressed such views if it hadn't been for Mr. Stubblebine and others who have been proposing drastic fiscal therapy.

BRUCE BARTLETT, Office of Senator Roger Jepson: When we hear talk about the biases in our system that lead to increased spending, the discussion is usually about political biases: people want more, but they don't want to pay for it. But I'm concerned about a different set of biases: those of the economics profession. I will loosely term them "Keynesian" biases, and they relate directly to the Congressional Budget Act. You see these biases in the econometric models that everybody uses to determine and project budget. You find, for example, that if you increase spending and taxes at the same time, this is good for the economy; if you cut taxes and spending at the same time, this is bad; and if you increase spending, this is better than reducing taxes. It is these kinds of biases that you get in all of the reports of the Congressional Budget Office. And as a result, there is a growing feeling among the people I have talked to that the Congressional Budget Act has been a failure precisely because it has justified the deficits ahead of time rather than having them be of an accidental nature, which was considered the basic problem with deficit spending prior to the Budget Act. And on the floor of the Senate, Senator Russell Long says that when he voted for the Budget Act, he thought he was voting for a balanced budget, but obviously it didn't happen. Would the panel comment?

MR. MCINTYRE: Is it your suggestion that if we had different people in the Congressional Budget Office our problem would be solved?

MR. BARTLETT: It would probably help a great deal.

MR. MCINTYRE: If you meant that the act is a problem, I can come to its defense. Unbelievable as it may sound, I think the Congressional Budget Act is a good thing and has had beneficial effects on the budget process. I'd be glad to expound on that.

PROFESSOR STEIN: I assumed the question had to do with the nature of econometric models that are used by the Congressional Budget Office and by most other forecasting agencies, commercial as well as governmental. My perception is that what you call biases do exist in short-range forecasting, which is all the models are good for. They always make it appear as though, with any assumption of unutilized resources, you get far more from a stimulus in real output at very little cost in terms of an inflationary bump than you actually do. And the same for the down side. There is a real risk in using econometric models as a projection device in that the short-run consequences can build themselves in in the longer run and become very misleading. If that is what you meant, I think you have made a valid challenge.

MR. BARTLETT: My question really concerns the consensus idea that a certain level of deficit is, by definition, good, based on whatever circumstances are put into the model. This is quite different from the process of putting together the budget in the past, where each committee operated on its own and there was no thought-out idea about what the deficit ought to be a year ahead of time. And as a result, I feel, there is a bias built into the present process: that you are always moving up to whatever the prejustified level of deficit is.

DR. BURNS: But do you mean to say that the Congressional Budget Act has resulted in deficits that are larger than they would have been in the absence of that legislation?

MR. BARTLETT: Yes.

MR. MCINTYRE: I seriously doubt that.

DR. BURNS: I am not as enthusiastic as Jim McIntyre is, but I do think the Congressional Budget Act has to some degree rationalized fiscal discussions in the Congress. It has even led to some reduction in spending; but that has been marginal, and in that sense I have been disappointed. I had expected much more from this legislation. Nevertheless, the act has been a modest, constructive force toward reducing government spending.

Rationalizing the budgetary process, so that revenues and expenditures are considered simultaneously, marks a considerable advance over what we had previously. As to the biases of congressmen and their staffs, I doubt whether the Congressional Budget Act has affected them. Things weren't any better in the past; I think they were worse.

MR. MCINTYRE: There is one area that I would describe as a problem because it risks misleading us, and unnecessarily so. The implementation of the Humphrey-Hawkins Act, if I understand it correctly, mandates that the OMB and the budget base their projections, out to five years, upon the totally incompatible and unrealistic assumptions of 4 percent unemployment with 3 percent inflation by 1983. This past year, the budget and the Council of Economic Advisers had to struggle to say something reasonable about the projections that were based upon those numbers. One way to improve the process of forecasting, since we are talking about the budget implications of a set of policies, would be to withdraw those constraints now written into law in the Humphrey-Hawkins Act.

ALLEN UNSWORTH, Budget Committee, House of Representatives: One formula that would get around some of the objections to requiring an annually balanced budget is the Rousselot-Armstrong bill. Under its provisions the budget could be unbalanced by a three-fifths vote of both houses for any reason. This avoids having to define a "national" or "economic emergency," which is required by the escape clauses in most other balanced budget bills or amendments.

The Rousselot-Armstrong bill also provides for income tax indexation, and would require income tax rate increases to be voted on explicitly by a three-fifths majority of both houses. This provision would eliminate the objection that there would be a bias toward balancing the budget by tax increases rather than by restraining expenditures.

I would appreciate the comments of any of the panelists on this approach.

PROFESSOR STUBBLEBINE: One of the things I suggested in my remarks is that there may be some as yet unexplored alternatives. The Rousselot-Armstrong amendment is one of those alternatives. I have no trouble with its provisions, but I prefer the spending limit amendment because of its greater flexibility. It does not try to mandate a result, but to establish incentives to produce a result. This is a superior approach to Rousselot-Armstrong, and that is the basis of my preference.

DR. BURNS: I have to speak in opposition to one part of your proposal—the part that calls for indexing of the income tax. I am opposed to any and every form of indexing for a very simple reason. When you start indexing, you say in effect that we are going to have inflation in the future and we therefore must learn how to live with it.

I do not accept that assumption. Inflation is an evil that must be fought. To the extent that we index anything—whether it be the income tax or social security or your salary or mine—we lost a part of the constituency that is still fighting against inflation.

If it were really possible to index everything—every form of payment, every price—I would not argue against it; but that is impossible. In arguing against every variety of indexing, I recognize of course that some elements of justice are being overlooked in the short run in the process.

ROBERT HARTMAN, The Brookings Institution: The major difference between the current congressional budget procedures and the statutory approach you suggest, Dr. Burns, seems to me to be the following: under existing procedures, if Congress does want to move toward budget balance or toward restraint, it has to spell out, function by function, where the restraint should take place—in its conference report, it has to spell out, committee by committee, what changes are needed to bring about the restraint. In contrast, a generalized statutory approach deals only with aggregates. It permits, in effect, a cheap vote on aggregates but does not really require any implementation at all. How can you be for such a thing?

DR. BURNS: I think of the kind of statute that I sketched as an amendment to the Congressional Budget Act. Therefore, nothing that is now being done under that act, in the way of examination of individual spending categories and laying down rules to be followed by the Congress, would be affected.

STEVE ENTIN, Joint Economic Committee, U.S. Congress: Just as an aside, the closer one gets to Capitol Hill in looking at the Budget Act, budget committees, budget resolutions, and the budget process, the less clothing the emperor or empress seems to be wearing.

DR. BURNS: The emperor is becoming more interesting, though, in the process.

MR. ENTIN: My basic question is this. We are dwelling on narrow economic questions in this discussion, but the call for a constitutional convention seems to me to be a call to restructure the institutional biases in the Congress. The diffuse interests of the majority who are being taxed and nickel-and-dimed to death are being pitted against the intense concentrated interests of the special groups who fight for their particular programs, the pressure by the press on members of Congress to appear to be active, the pressure on congressional staffs to look busy and to make their members look active. Congress has no incentive at all to change these biases, and this is why the public is moving toward a call for a constitutional convention.

On the economic side, isn't it really pretty weak to oppose a constitutional approach on the grounds that it lacks flexibility or by repeating the myth that the current system acts as an automatic stabilizer in a period of inflation? It is widely understood now that under a spending limit, you could still have a Keynesian form of stimulus in the form of a bigger deficit by cutting taxes. Under a balanced budget amendment, if you were habitually running surpluses, you could have a Keynesian stimulus simply by dropping a lower surplus. So, really, how strong is the economic argument of the opponents here, and how strong is the public's move toward changing the institutional bias in Congress in a way it will not do itself?

PROFESSOR JAMES BUCHANAN, Virginia Polytechnic Institute: I am very disappointed, actually, in the tone of this discussion because it is too oriented toward Washington. Except for Dr. Burns and, of course, Professor Stubblebine, there has been no sense of what might be happening "out there"—the reaction of the people to what is going on. I hear economic explanations and economic discussions, and, to be sure, one can tear all these proposals up and down, and across the middle, and every which way—from the perspective in Washington. But the country is not Washington.

I was accused in the first session of bringing up the people, but let me bring up the people again. The people are exercised about what is going on, but I do not hear much discussion here about what is going to happen if we just leave it at hoping things will get a little better. I am sure Mr. McIntyre and the administration and Congress, with the best of intentions, planned a balance, but the people don't trust them anymore. They just don't trust them anymore.

I think Dr. Burns is on absolutely the right track. Something drastic has to be done. If it is not done this way, it will be done some other way. To be sure, this is a popular prejudice, and some popular prejudices are bad. But it seems to me this gives a chance to seize the day. I am

73

in favor of any and every one of these amendments, whichever one happens to prevail, simply because the people are exercised. Something must be done, or else we are just going down the road to destroying our country in a very big hurry.

That is a good term, *drastic therapy*. The symbolism of drastic therapy has already had a big effect—Dr. Burns is absolutely right. But discussion of drastic therapy is not enough. I think the symbolism of something like the balanced budget amendment would have dramatic effects. It would have dramatic effects on the situation of the dollar. It would have dramatic effects on people's expectations. This dimension seems to be missing in this sort of enclosed Washington atmosphere, if I may say so.

MR. MCINTYRE: You argue that the end justifies the means, the end being a balanced budget no matter how you get there. I question that philosophy. Whatever you think ought to be done, somebody else will think just the opposite. We do live in a democracy, and we have to shape a consensus. And I would agree with Dr. Burns: focusing the debate on balancing the budget has been extremely helpful to me in carrying out my mission.

If you really want to do something about fiscal responsibility, tackle federal spending. Payments to individuals amount to about $250 billion, almost half the budget. That figure is increasing rapidly, and it is going to increase more rapidly. Why? The population is getting older. People are retiring and drawing retirement benefits and Medicare benefits. And another major federal expenditure, national health insurance, looms on the horizon, whether you are for it or against it.

If you really want to do something about fiscal responsibility, then focus attention on what we are going to do ten or twenty years from now about those big programs. We will be financing social security out of a smaller work force in the future. These big programs will be serious problems, in my judgment.

I am not an economist, by the way. This is fortunate in many respects because it gives me a different perspective on the budget and budget policy, although I find economists who make sure that I do not deviate from some of the well-founded principles. But still, my perspective is that it is easy to talk about and to get support for the general objective of balancing the budget, but we have to deal with persistent claims for exceptions, and most of them have some merit. So we have to learn to say no, and we have to learn to make priorities, and that is why I think the Congressional Budget Act is important—for this one simple reason. Under the old process, nobody looked at the totals. Now we set some totals and then debate the priorities within those totals. I submit that this is a significant, fundamental change in the way Congress goes about deciding on the budget.

So focus on federal spending because, if you do that, the tax side will take care of itself automatically. That is my challenge to people who want to balance the budget.

MR. MACLAURY: The charge that we in this room are Washingtonians and therefore deaf is really not fair. The music out there is being heard: the frustration and, indeed, anger of the taxpayers are having an impact. Congress is going through the budget process this year with a wholly different ethos from ever before as a result of Proposition 13. Brookings sponsored a session for new members of Congress in January, and I can tell you that those people felt that they had been sent here specifically with a mandate to cut expenditures. They were very frustrated and intemperate with those who tried to tell them, as Mr. McIntyre did just now, how difficult it is to do. So there is no doubt the word is getting through to Washington. The question, it seems to me, is how long shall we rattle the saber, which is how I see this constitutional amendment discussion. Are we really going to unsheathe the saber and thrust it home? That is the real debate.

SPENCER REIBMAN, Office of Congressman John Rousselot: It seems to me that Messrs. McIntyre and MacLaury are making an eloquent defense of Professor Stubblebine's tax limitation amendment. Milton Friedman testified before the House Judiciary Committee recently, and he said that the problem Congress faces now in trying to cut the budget is that there is a "give me" predisposition. Everybody is on the take. Everybody wants more. If you had a tax limitation, or some sort of requirement that ends the free ride that inflation and the tax code now give Congress, then, as Professor Friedman argues, when it comes time to spend, Congress would have to set clear priorities and not let new expenditures slip into the budget as a lot of new expenditures slip in now. So, therefore, the points that Messrs. MacLaury and McIntyre are making really seem to argue in favor of some sort of a balanced budget or tax limitation approach.

But then in an about-face, it seems that Mr. McIntyre is saying that the economy is not yet ready for a balanced budget. We have first to primp the economy, get the economic bedding set up, make the bed, see that the pillows are nice and fluffed, and then we can slide in for a soft landing. But intentionally slowing down the economy, the administration's stated objective, to defeat inflation may not result in a soft landing. It may result in a hard recession, with high inflation.

Slowing the economy by gradually pushing taxpayers into higher

75

tax brackets could have disastrous repercussions. As the tax rates rise and the money supply increases, the tax burden in the economy increases because of bracket creep. As a result, the rate of economic growth is likely to decline because productivity will inevitably fall off. Then, Mr. McIntyre, you will probably have an increase in the price level, and you will never achieve your soft landing because inflationary expectations, as Dr. Burns pointed out, will increase.

So I am not sure whether I understand the administration's rationale for trying to slow the economy as a prerequisite to a balanced budget. I understand the administration believes that we suffer from inflation because there is not enough resource slack in the economy, but there is strong evidence to suggest that there is no relationship between inflation and the rate of capacity utilization—a measure of resource slack—or for that matter, inflation and unemployment.

PROFESSOR STUBBLEBINE: Mr. Reibman said it for me. Messrs. MacLaury and McIntyre have made the case for an amendment—for precisely the reasons that statutory policies will not work in the long run. In fact, the main danger of Proposition 13 and the scurrying of politicians to respond to it is that, having balanced the budget by 1980 or 1981 by holding down spending, they will be inclined to rest on their laurels. And once the dust begins to settle, we will go back to business as usual; and then five or ten or twenty years from now, we will be back meeting again, discussing whether we should have a constitutional amendment to try to deal with the increase in government spending and inflation.

The statutory limitations sound good until the crunch comes—when all the demands for increased government spending begin to pile up in the halls of the Congress. That will test the limits of the statutory provisions.

Politicians are reeling under Proposition 13 now, but I have no doubt that they will be able to recover their equilibrium and go back to doing things as they did before. That is why we need a constitutional amendment—the reason is as pure and simple as that.

Part Three

Constitutional Restrictions on the
Power of the Purse and the Theory of
Public Choice

Introduction

Rudolph G. Penner, Chairman

The whole movement for an amendment is a people's movement, in the sense that it has sprung up from below. It is fair to say that it has caught politicians and, to some degree, academics by surprise. But we are fortunate today to have as speakers a very high proportion of the people in this world who have been giving long thought to the issues raised by the notion of using constitutional amendments to change the way we make decisions.

Procedural and Quantitative Constitutional Constraints on Fiscal Authority

James M. Buchanan

Economists of the garden variety seem to have little or nothing to contribute to the discussion of the various proposals to impose constitutional limits on the powers of government to tax and to spend. This is paradoxical, since clearly the basic impact of the proposals would be, and is intended to be, economic. But most economists are inhibited because constitutional "policy," as distinct from ordinary legislative policy, lies outside their familiar framework for discussion. Economists are usually quite willing to advise or to criticize officials in making ordinary, postconstitutional policy. But constitutional constraints are viewed negatively because they would necessarily restrict the ability of policy makers to follow the proffered advice of economists.

Public choice economists, those of us who have concerned ourselves with the processes of political decision making, are at some advantage in confronting issues of constitutional policy. Of necessity, collective decisions must be made through some process, some rules for combining separate individual values or preferences, whether of voters, groups, parties, or members of legislative assemblies. And such rules are necessarily "constitutional" in the sense that they are chosen separately from and independently of the particular choices we might make on particular issues. Indeed, these rules are presumed to remain invariable over a whole sequence of separate policy issues. In our initial work on what may be called an "economic theory of the political constitution," Gordon Tullock and I concentrated on the choice of decision rules. In this, we were following the lead of Knut Wicksell, who looked to economic policy reform through reform of the constitutional decision rules through which economic policy emerges. However, neither Wicksell nor Tullock and I fully explored the possible substitutability between decision rules and other kinds of constitutional constraints intended for comparable purposes.

Before discussing possible substitutability, I should emphasize that any constitution, any set of rules selected independently of the particularized choice setting, necessarily restricts the range of options available to the decision-making unit, whether this be an individual, a committee, a firm, or a legislative assembly. The very purpose of rules, of constitutions, is to prevent us from making decisions in an overemotional or overpragmatic response to particular situations. Constitutional choices are presumably made at a more "rational" level of consideration, with situational distractions at least partially subordinated to long-term interests. Constitutional choice in politics is analogous to the long-run planning decision familiar in the neoclassical theory of the firm, whereas postconstitutional choice is akin to short-run output decisions. The short-run options are necessarily constrained by the prior long-run commitments.

Now let me return to the specific issue of fiscal limits—proposed constitutional constraints on governmental powers to tax and to spend. We have always had such constraints in our political history, although economists, for the most part, have ignored them. The very institution of taxation, for instance, stems from the acknowledged constitutional constraint against arbitrary discrimination in "taking" resources from citizens without due process of law and without due compensation. If government could simply take what it needs, why should it bother to tax? Further, even within the taxing power, governments are further prohibited from arbitrary discrimination. As we know, a *constitutional* amendment was required, the Sixteenth, to grant government the discriminatory tax treatment embodied in the progressive income tax.

Those who favor additional constraints are, therefore, merely proposing that we add to the constitutional constraints that exist and that have always existed. But why are additional constraints considered to be necessary? This question brings me back to the relationship I mentioned earlier between constitutional rules for decision making and constitutional rules on the powers to tax and spend. The need for additional fiscal constraints did not become apparent until the empirical-historical record began to suggest that the nonfiscal constraints had failed. Nineteenth- and twentieth-century political thought, as expressed by scholar and citizen alike, embodied a blind faith that, somehow, the competitive pressures of electoral politics made explicit consideration of further constitutional constraints unnecessary. That is to say, the prevailing mythology about politics was that, so long as politicians and political parties were required to submit their record to the voters periodically, the overall results could not really get out of bounds. "Democracy at work" meant government by congressional majorities, and any constraint on majorities' freedom to work their will could only reduce the flexibility of response to "needs." (This attitude was expressed clearly by Justice Felix Frankfurter with respect to economic legislation.) The very notion of what I have elsewhere called the "constitutional atti-

81

tude"—the vision of the Founding Fathers of a society in which government, too, would be kept strictly within *constitutional* limits—was lost to the consciousness of the dominant American political mind.

Fortunately, in my view, residues of such an attitude had not entirely disappeared. And the accumulating fiscal record in the decades after World War II suggested that government had clearly overstepped any reasonable bounds. Even the most ardent defender of public sector growth is hard put to account for the post-1965 explosion, in particular, solely in terms of a democracy's response to the demands of the citizenry. Increasingly, the growth patterns came to be understood and interpreted as the outputs of a political sector that has an internal dynamic of its own, subject to relatively indirect and incomplete electoral control.

The time came, in the late 1970s, for a reassessment of constitutional limits. Again, the prospect for two different approaches should be recognized. Wicksell wanted to allow full flexibility in tax-sharing schemes, but he wanted to require more than simple majorities for spending authorizations. He also wanted to reform the decision processes in legislatures to require simultaneous consideration of items of spending and of the taxing necessary to finance them. Wicksell wanted legislators to be forced to confront the benefits and the costs of each spending proposal on its own.

As we know, Congress itself recognized that its own processes had got out of hand and passed the Budget Reform Act of 1974 in an attempt to restore some order. But this was legislative rather than constitutional reform: Its long-term results cannot be estimated, and it takes little or no political sophistication to recognize that the structure through which fiscal decisions are made is a long way from the Wicksellian ideal. Many of the proposed constitutional limits can, therefore, be interpreted as attempts to modify procedures so as to move closer to Wicksell's ideal, where taxing and spending decisions would, indeed, reflect rational benefit-cost responses to citizens' demands for government action. Alan Greenspan, among others, has called for two-thirds majorities on all spending legislation, clearly a Wicksellian reform; and the neglected part of Proposition 13 also calls for a qualified legislative majority for the enactment of new taxes.

The balanced budget amendment can also be interpreted in these terms. Considered at its simplest, this proposal is based on the readily understood notion that governmental decision making should be required, in the large, to balance out the two sides of the account. Indeed, the widespread support for this proposal stems from its place in citizens' logical understanding of their own affairs. Interestingly enough, budget balance was a part of the pre-Keynesian fiscal constitution, even if it was implicit rather than explicit. The effect of Keynesian economic policy was to destroy this part of the fiscal constitution. Keynesian economics told politicians that deficits were good. Since politicians always want to spend and never to tax, the regime of deficits followed. The amendment is an attempt to undo much of the resulting damage. Since I have written a book on this, I shall not elaborate the argument here.

Another existing procedural constraint, one that has historical-legal origins in the U.S. Constitution, is the legal recognition of the federal structure, with units at each level being assigned and restricted to the exercise of specific fiscal powers. This and other procedural constraints have in common that they seek, not to operate upon specific outcomes, but to modify the processes or rules through which fiscal decisions are made. Clearly, there is some relationship between the procedural reforms suggested and the directions of change in the predicted sequence of results. But procedural reforms do have the advantage that they do not directly restrict the potential for response to the demands of citizens, either in relative or in absolute terms. None of the procedural constraints places a ceiling on the share of GNP that might be collected in taxes or appropriated for public or governmental use.

It is precisely this characteristic that distinguishes the procedural from the quantitative constraints that have been variously proposed. If the processes through which governments make budgetary decisions are considered not amenable to constitutional change, because amendments either may not pass or may not be effective if they did pass, then attempts to impose constitutional constraints more directly on the results may seem justifiable.

The set of proposals that seem to have gained widest favor among the subset of economists who support any constitutional changes falls within this category. These are proposals to impose constitutional limits on the share of income and/or product that might be collected in taxes or expended for public uses, or, alternatively, to set limits on the increase in this share in relationship to increases in income and/or product. This set of proposals has the apparent advantage of bypassing or ignoring the processes through which fiscal results might be generated within the governmental structure. Their disadvantage lies in the rigidity they would necessarily impose on the potential response to demands. In recognition of this disadvantage, most specific proposals of the share or ratio type embody escape clauses which allow departure from the constraint by a modified decision rule. In total, therefore, these proposals embody both quantitative and procedural limits.

Geoffrey Brennan and I have found, in analyzing alternative constitutional constraints on fiscal powers, that constraints on the bases for taxation allowed to government may have much to recommend them. These constraints allow for flexibility in response to spending demands within relatively wide limits, but at the same time, act to keep government's fiscal appetites within certain limits.

The quantitative constraint that is most widely known is, of course, Proposition 13—the constitutional lid imposed on California real property tax rates. An advantage, and indeed one of the success secrets of this sort of constraint, lies in its directness. An offsetting disadvantage is its rigidity with regard to rates, along with the accompanying temptation offered to governments to choose other tax bases and to shift fiscal responsibility upward to higher-level units.

This brief review of some of the proposals for constitutional fiscal constraints, though cast in general terms, has probably revealed my own attitudes toward them. I support almost any and all proposals, and I would not reject any proposal on the ground that there may be better ways to accomplish similar results. It seems to me that the need for constraining government is so urgent that we must capitalize on the momentum that Proposition 13 has set off.

Constitutional Limitations as Self-denying Ordinances

William H. Riker

In order to explain the motive for a constitutional limitation on spending, I would like to convince you that it is perfectly possible for a group of people to vote themselves into a worse position than they were in to start with. We might call this a Pareto pessimal result, in contrast to the Pareto optimal results of markets, and I will set up here a situation where it could happen. Then I will show that if the group divides itself into sections that elect representatives to a legislature, then the chances of its voting itself into a worse position than before are even greater—a doubly Pareto pessimal result. Some recent discoveries in social choice theory suggest that these twin results are not just pitfalls in my fertile imagination; they are almost certain to occur in the real world. These unfortunate features of voting systems are the motive for constitutional limitations on spending and go a long way toward justifying them.

To begin with, consider a group of people, numbering 3 or 80 million, who consider adopting by majority vote a set of, say, 100 sentences. These sentences, if and once adopted, change the rules for interaction within the group and are thus exactly like statutes. Of course, one thing the group might decide to do with these sentences is reject them all. For the purposes of my story, I assume that the sentences are such that this is exactly what isolated, myopic, self-interested people would do. By "isolated" I mean the people do not communicate or make binding agreements. By "myopic" I mean that they look only at the immediate benefit from a single sentence and neither at long-term benefits nor at the benefits of several sentences taken together. By "self-interested" I mean that each person bases his or her decision only on a guess about whether the sentence would benefit him or her (economically, emotionally, or ideologically).

I hasten to point out that my null model is not unrealistic. We have all seen voters reject a whole set of referenda or a legislature reject all or most of an executive program. Of course, I doubt very much that a truly isolated, myopic, self-interested electorate ever existed, but there are enough of these characteristics in the world to treat this as at least one extreme of possible situations.

To make this model work in such a way that the 100 sentences are in fact adopted, I assume that the voters may be divided into three categories with regard to each one of the sentences. The first is supporters—those who benefit from the adoption of the sentence. This category is by definition a minority because I have assumed that isolated, myopic, self-interested voters would reject every one of the sentences. Furthermore, since this minority has to be the driving force in transforming a losing sentence into a winning one, I must assume that benefits for this group are great enough to inspire the members to work hard for adoption. A second group with regard to each sentence is its strong opponents—those who are seriously harmed by its adoption. This category must also be a minority because, were it a majority, there would be no hope whatever of adopting the sentence.

The pivots are those who are mildly harmed by the adoption of a sentence. The people in this category, while opposed, can be persuaded to support it if they are appropriately compensated. Since the first two categories counteract each other, this third category of mildly opposed is pivotal in the sense that it can decide the outcome. An example of supporters is producers of cane and beet sugar who deeply desire a subsidy; an example of opponents is candy manufacturers; and an example of pivots is household consumers who buy only a few pounds of sugar per year.

Now consider two sentences that have the following features: The category of strong opponents of one sentence includes the category of strong opponents of the other. Consequently, if both sentences were adopted, these people would be doubly hurt. On the other hand, the supporters of the two sentences, while mutually exclusive categories, are not strong opponents of either sentence. That is, the strong supporters of sentence 1 are pivots on sentence 2 and the strong supporters of sentence 2 are pivots on sentence 1. Here we have the basis for a coalition to pass both sentences. By promising to ensure the adoption of sentence 2, the strong supporters of sentence 1 (who are pivots on sentence 2) obtain the help of the pivots on sentence 1 (who are strong supporters of sentence 2) to adopt sentence 1. And by the same agreement, the strong supporters of sentence 2 ensure its adoption. Both categories thus gain considerably from the coalition at only a modest cost.

If such a situation exists and people are allowed to communicate and make agreements, as must happen, of course, in any democratic system, then one can expect that these 2 of the 100 sentences will pass. If this were the end of the matter, it would simply be that members of two minorities had bettered themselves at the expense of another minority. It might be argued that this is an unfair imposition on the losers;

but, since the successful minorities are together a majority, one can hardly denounce the outcome as a violation of democratic morality.

But to carry my story further, let us now suppose that there are two more sentences such that the losers on the first two sentences are strong supporters of sentence 3 and pivots on sentence 4, while supporters of, say, sentence 2 are also supporters of sentence 4 and pivots on sentence 3. Here exists the basis for a coalition to adopt sentences 3 and 4. One can carry the matter further by assuming an appropriate distribution of interests and show that coalitions can be constructed to pass all or most of the 100 sentences.

I have already assumed that, without such coalitions, none of the sentences would pass. It is not a big step then to imagine further that, for each person in the group, the absolute sum of what each loses when he or she is in the minority on a pair of sentences is greater than what he or she wins when in the majority on a pair of sentences. Indeed, it is easy to construct examples in dollars or any other measure in which exactly this happens. This is a unanimity of misery, truly a Pareto pessimal result, in which *everybody* is worse off than before the coalition building and voting began. The situation is an example of what has been variously named the prisoners' dilemma or the tragedy of the commons.

It might be thought that reasonable people would avoid this result simply by agreeing not to adopt any of the sentences. But such an agreement is not easy to make or to keep because each person knows that enforcement is difficult and that everyone else has an incentive to break the agreement. The problem of the 100 sentences is thus very much like the problem of avoiding the extinction of whales and at least as difficult to resolve.

Indeed, the problem of the sentences is probably even harder to solve because statutes are usually adopted by legislatures rather than by referenda or town meetings. Ordinary members of the voting group have only the incentives inherent in the sentences themselves to bring about the Pareto pessimal result, but legislators have in addition a personal motive to adopt the sentences. The legislator is, in a sense, a broker in the construction of coalitions, and he or she gets a kind of broker's fee. Hence, the dilemma of the sentences is exacerbated when it occurs in the legislative setting.

Suppose the supporters of two sentences are concentrated in a few constituencies while the strong opponents of these sentences are either concentrated in other constituencies or scattered about fairly evenly. In such a circumstance, the legislators from the districts with strong supporters can get a lot of popular credit by brokering the necessary coalition while generating very little resentment. The people in the pivotal category are not hurt as much by the sentence on which they lose as they benefit from the sentence on which they win. Hence, they are not likely to resent the loss or to punish the legislator. Indeed, in many real-world examples, the loss is so relatively small that losers barely notice it. Given this circumstance, the broker-legislators build up credit with segments of their constituencies by repeated coalition building, thus acting out the conventional picture of democratic representation. A powerful private motive, reelection, encourages all legislators to adopt all 100 sentences. It has become common lately among liberal students of Congress to say that legislators *consciously* bedevil the society simply to set up a situation for which they can then earn electoral credits by providing remedies. By my account, however, they need not be consciously Machiavellian: the creation of coalitions to pass undesired sentences is merely a rational response to the electoral situation.

Such is my model of a situation where Pareto pessimal results can occur. Nothing in this model, however, suggests how frequently such situations might arise. Are they a remote fantasy or a very real and frequent horror?

Between these two extremes, I believe that events in the real world are closer to the horror than the fantasy. Classic examples of building coalitions to adopt 100 undesired sentences are the passage of tariff acts, rivers and harbors bills, etc. To give a contemporary example, consider subsidies for sugar. Only a small minority of citizens in any state (except Hawaii) benefits from this subsidy. Although the minority is tiny, it is nevertheless concentrated in about a half-dozen sugar- beet-producing states and three cane-producing states. Its influence is therefore magnified into a substantial bloc of legislators, who are extremely conscious of the electoral significance for themselves of satisfying this producer interest.

The group of strong opponents are refiners of imported cane sugar, candy manufacturers, and, until recently, soft drink bottlers. This group is, however, spread so widely about that it cannot influence any legislators very much. Of course, nearly everybody in his or her role as consumer is hurt doubly by subsidies for sugar. They pay the subsidy through taxes and then pay the high prices for the sugar itself. But sugar is not a large item in any consumer's budget. Hence the representatives of consumers are pivots. With just a bit of hurt on sugar, they can generate advantages on other items. I do not suggest that the sugar congressmen and senators actually make deals on the subsidy. Rather, there is a whole agriculture program into which their interest fits. In line with the wisdom in the phrase "to get along, go along," the several kinds of agricultural and partisan interests involved go along with sugar and thereby get their own subsidies on cotton, corn, or whatever. It is easily demonstrable that nearly everyone is hurt by the sugar subsidy because it has turned out in the last few years to be economically feasible to build huge refining plants for corn sweeteners. That it is feasible to substitute for sugar a product that costs about twice as much to produce as cane sugar itself, is, it seems to me, sufficient evidence that a lot of people are worse off for the subsidy; yet the subsidy persists.

Without going into the detail of many examples, I think a similar case could be made about most of the tax code, about most of the subsidies to state governments, and on and on. And there is a good reason why this is so.

One of the most striking recent discoveries of social choice theory is that, given several dimensions of judgment, the chance of an equilibrium from majority voting is close to zero. By equilibrium I mean a sentence or a platform or a motion that can beat all its alternatives. Such an equilibrium outcome is often called a Condorcet winner or a core. The first part of the discovery is that the conditions necessary for an equilibrium to exist in the real world are so hard to satisfy that one would never expect it to occur. The second part is that, once equilibrium breaks down, it breaks down completely so that there is a way to pass by majority vote every conceivable sentence platform or motion. Whether a sentence is passed is determined by the path one takes to get to it—the sequence by which alternatives are eliminated—as much as by the preferences of the members of the society.

The meaning of this astonishing discovery is that one would ordinarily expect the outcome of voting to be somewhat unsatisfactory in terms of the interests of the majority. And it is precisely this situation that proposals for constitutional limitations on spending are intended to remedy.

Given that nearly anything can pass, one way to avoid a Pareto pessimal result is to prohibit ahead of time, if possible, some of the worst of potential outcomes. One of these worst outcomes is a result we see in nearly every country, a huge long-term growth in the public sector. In the nineteenth century, growth of this sector was inhibited by ideological constraints, but these have been lost in this century. We have, I believe, been trying to find a substitute constraint for some time now. Program budgeting, sunset laws, zero-based budgeting, the congressional budget resolution, are all devices aimed at some kind of prohibition of Pareto pessimal outcomes in appropriations. And it is not strange that we should try these devices. The usual solution to prisoners' dilemmas or tragedies of the commons is some sort of self-denying ordinance. This is precisely what the proposed constitutional limitations on spending are, self-denying ordinances just like the other constraints that have been tried. It is possible, even likely, that the constitutional limitations will not work any better than these other constraints have. It is typical that agreements to resolve prisoners' dilemmas are broken time and again until a satisfactory solution is found. So it would be reasonable to expect, for example, that spending limitations have the result that legislators, finding themselves unable to spend, enact laws to require private persons to do the spending for them. If that happens, then additional constitutional limitations will be necessary. In any event, if I am right that excessive public spending is a Pareto pessimal result in a huge prisoners' dilemma, then we will continue to search for some kind of self-denying ordinance until a successful one is found.

Is the Balanced Budget Amendment Another Form of Prohibition?

Mancur Olson

A common approach in our society, as in others, to a social or economic problem, is to pass a law against the evil or to set up a government program to alleviate it. A classic example is the Eighteenth Amendment to the Constitution—prohibition as a reaction to the problem of drunkenness. This amendment did, for a time, limit the amount of alcohol consumed, but it also had some unintended and unfortunate side effects. One was that people sometimes got very bad bootleg booze, which caused problems greater than those caused by consuming the kind of alcoholic beverages one could get in a society where they were legal. Another unhappy side effect, of course, was a lot of crime, even organized crime, and probably a diminution in the respect for law.

Another example of the social tendency to outlaw or to enact a program against an evil is the use of price control during periods of inflation. People do not like the higher prices, and so they say, "Let us have a price and wage freeze." And the freeze will perhaps, for a time anyway, keep down at least some prices and wages. But, of course, the price and wage freeze does not deal with the problem that led to the inflation any more than prohibition dealt with the social and personal problems that drove people to drink.

And so, in some suppressed form, in some different form, inflation continues. The price and wage controls are increasingly evaded as time goes on, because evasion is very profitable. The increase in demand that drove the inflation now manifests itself, particularly in cases where prices do not rise, in long queues and shortages. I believe there are hundreds of examples of cases where our society has seen some kind of problem, tried to ban it or deal with it by some legislative change, and then found that the banning or the legislative change not only failed to work in the long run, but also brought an extra burden.

As may have already been assumed, I am going to suggest that many advocates of balanced budget amendments are trying to deal with excessive government spending and with inflation by a method that is analogous to prohibition and to wage and price control. They reason that because excessive government spending and inflation are social evils, we must outlaw them. And, of course, a law to constrain the Congress and the president would have to be a constitutional amendment.

But, just as the demand for alcohol persisted and the profits for supplying alcohol persisted even under prohibition, and just as the demand for goods under a price and wage freeze remains high if the monetary and fiscal policy that generated the inflation persists; so the demands of voters and pressure groups for whatever they have been demanding will not disappear just because a constitutional amendment bans deficit financing. One cannot ban the ingenuity of politicians and bureaucrats, who advance their own careers by satisfying the demands of pressure groups and the electorate. So I do not think we will achieve a lot by constitutional amendments to control budget deficits. If the forces that make for these deficits remain, the problems will continue to be with us in one way or another.

Furthermore, a constitutional amendment would entail the same sort of excess burden, the same sort of unintended side effects, that have followed from other attempts at banning. For instance, we can predict that an effective limitation on government deficits would encourage politicians to pass regulations, the social cost of which is borne by the private sector. One such case might involve damming a river to control water levels and thus pollution levels. If the dam could not be built out of the government budget, then the government might require the private sector to deal with the problem, even in circumstances where this is not efficient. The total social costs in this instance would be greater under the balanced budget limitation than without it.

Another possible side effect is a distortion of capital expenditures in the federal budget. A balanced budget amendment would probably make reasonable arrangements for capital expenditures. But in many cases, capital expenditures are hard to distinguish from current expenditures, and it might very well happen that lots of current expenditures would be classified as capital expenditures. As a result, the pattern of government expenditures would be distorted in an inefficient way under an effective balanced budget amendment.

Also, it seems to me, we should be cautious about demanding too much of our Constitution, given that it is a precious and, I believe, a fragile thing. The respect we have for the Constitution is a function of, among other things, the extent to which we are in the habit of following it. To use the scarce resource of our constitutional inhibition to fight the powerful tendencies in our political and economic system for government spending and for deficits is to endanger that scarce resource. The continent just south of us is full of countries which have, several times, had constitutions quite like our own and not managed to keep them.

Some may find my point of view on the proposed amendments puzzling because many people see the problem very differently. One reason for this is that when we study the history of our country, we may not always inoculate ourselves against the disease of assuming that all our national achievements are due to the character of our Constitution. The United States Constitution is probably the most successful of all government constitutions, and it *has* played a role in our country's achievements. But we must realize that the United States has had some other things going for it besides.

One reason the framers wrote the kind of constitution they did was the balance of power among the states at the time. I am quite sure that one reason why our Constitution limits the power of the federal government is that many states would not have joined if it had not. The need to win the agreement of sovereign states constrained the Constitution to an incredible extent. And further, it surely constrained the government after the Constitution had been ratified. The Constitution made no provision for judicial review, but that sprang up very soon. One of the reasons it sprang up and persisted was that the country remained highly diversified, with many centers of power spread out over a vast area.

If we look at other countries, we find that their emphasis on written constitutions tends to be less, because they have not had our very unusual success with a written constitution. Nor do other countries share our somewhat exaggerated historiography of a constitution, our tendency to exaggerate its contribution to the country's success. Looking at other countries, particularly those with dramatically different constitutional structures, we generally find that the constitutional differences rest on prior differences in the character of the societies.

Suppose we ask why it is that France and Switzerland have such very different constitutions—the French with centralized power and essentially no local government; the Swiss with almost no central government but tremendous amounts of local autonomy. Is it that there were constitutional thinkers in France who believed in centralization, and constitutional thinkers in Switzerland who believed in decentralization? Not at all. The centralization of France began under the nationalist kings and continued under Napoleon; it has had obvious military, geographic, and cultural explanations. Similarly, the very limited central government of the Swiss rests on the fact that that mountainous region is filled with people who speak different languages, follow different religions, and are very jealous of their local powers.

What I am suggesting is that one cannot just write a new constitution for the French that would make them behave like the Swiss, or a new constitution for the Swiss that would make them behave like the French. Nor can one write a constitutional amendment for the United States that would make us behave much differently from the way we behave now, because the Constitution itself rests on a more fundamental reality. And while the Constitution may influence the underlying reality to a more than negligible extent, it is not by any means the sole determinant of that reality.

We must, in other words, not only avoid Marxian economic determinism but also avoid constitutional determinism. We must realize that constitutions do matter, but not only constitutions matter.

Would a Constitutional Amendment Limit Regulation and Inflation?

Anthony Downs

In preparing for this meeting, I took the approach of my friend Victor Palmieri, who used to moderate the television program "The Advocates," which was a debate on various issues. When he first started moderating, he would read all about these various issues in advance and come in as an expert, so that he could moderate and ask questions of both sides. But he discovered later that the best approach was to read nothing. He needed only to listen to what was presented in the debate, and to react to that.

This is exactly what I have done. I have listened to what has been said here. I came with no preconceived notions, prepared to react to the revealed wisdom of the true sages in this field, of whom I am not one. My remarks will have to be considered tentative, because I have not devoted much time to thinking about them. I found myself writing what I was going to say before Professor Olson got started, and I was in almost complete agreement with many things he said.

The speakers have convinced me that the question of whether restraints should be constitutional or legislative should not be viewed as a matter of principle, but as a matter of result. Professor Buchanan pointed out that we have had all kinds of constraints in the past, and the question is not really whether there is some principle that says which issues should or should not be dealt with constitutionally, but rather what will the results ultimately be. I suppose, in the long run, all principles are based on results, too, although it has been said there are times when a person must rise above principles. I do not think this is one of them. The question should be judged on the basis of the outcomes of adopting the various amendments in relation to the problems that stimulated the desire to amend. That causes me to look at what has stimulated people to desire to adopt the constitutional amendments we are discussing.

One of them is clearly the perceived growing role of government in the society. The other one, I believe, is inflation. Therefore, the key question is whether the adoption of amendments will in fact reduce or respond to these sources of dissatisfaction more effectively than alter-

95

native arrangements, particularly the ones we already have, or ones we could achieve without adopting constitutional amendments.

In regard to the role of government, Vice President Mondale once said, while he was still a senator, that even though he was a very liberal person and believed in government action in many spheres of life, his constituents were constantly complaining to him that the government was interfering in more and more aspects of their lives. Now, what is the nature of this interference? If one looks at the share of the *federal* budget in GNP, there has not been any startling increase over a period when people seemed at first to be satisfied with the present Constitution and later were not. I might mention a book just put out by the Brookings Institution, called *Setting National Priorities for the 1980 Budget*. In it is a table that shows that the federal budget share of GNP was 18.5 percent in 1960. It rose to a maximum of 22.6 percent in 1976 and in 1978 was 22.8 percent. Although this is an increase, I do not take it to be a startling revelation of government's expanding to a leviathan size during the past few years.

On the other hand, state and local government has expanded very significantly in that period, much more strikingly than the federal government in terms of both total expenditures and personnel. This is undoubtedly part of the cause of people's feeling that government is playing a larger role in their lives. Would a constitutional amendment, either the balanced budget or the federal spending limitation, do much about that?

It might, to some degree, because a lot of the expansion of state and local government lately has been supported by federal transfer payments. Forty percent or more of each city government's budget comes from intergovernmental transfers, mostly from the states, and the states collect far more from the federal government than they pass on to local governments. If we do away with the 40 percent of local government that is financed by the federal government, that is one way to get at the expansion of government in our lives.

Probably the most pernicious expansion of government activity, however, is the one Professor Olson mentioned. That is the expansion of regulation, rather than expenditures. And, in fact, in many government agencies, it is the restriction of their budgets in relation to their responsibilities that causes them to devise regulations that put the cost of achieving their regulatory objectives onto the private sector.

What accounts for the desire for regulation? What gives rise to that desire and to the generally expanding role of government as a whole, including state and local as well as federal government, in our society, is the increasing importance of externalities in a complicated society marked by interdependent actions among people and a high degree of urbanization. Externalities, as you know from economics, are not very well served by market transactions. It was long thought—and I believe I was one of the contributors to attacking this thought—that when a market fails to deal properly with an externality, the proper response is to turn it over to government because somehow the government will properly deal with it. That conclusion is incorrect, because the government may do worse at treating the externality than the private sector does. Nevertheless, it is the dissatisfaction with the results of purely market-oriented transactions, or dominantly market-oriented transactions, that gives rise initially to the desire for additional government action in the society. And I think that this cause of increased government activity is not going to be removed by any constitutional amendments of any kind whatever.

As Professor Olson pointed out, the desire for drinking was not removed by the prohibition amendment. And no amendment will eliminate the desire of people to have some kind of effective response to externalities that they believe are harming their lives. And yet there is a perception, which I think is very widespread, that there is too much interference in our lives from government regulation of all types. But the way to get at the regulatory problem is not to pass a constitutional amendment against federal spending, or rising federal spending, or deficits, or anything else. It is to deal more intelligently with the specific issues of regulation and with the politics of those issues as they come up in each case.

For example, consider the EPA's regulations on what kind of equipment must be used to remove the sulfur content of coal. The Ohio and West Virginia coal miners, who mine very high-sulfur coal, were afraid they would be put out of business by western coal, which is much lower in sulfur content. So they put political pressure on the administration to set standards which require all power plants to use the latest technology, regardless of what kind of coal they are using as an input. In other words, the cost of using any kind of coal would be extremely high. Many power companies could achieve the same air quality results by not using any equipment at all, but just shifting to western coal, but that, of course, would put the Ohio and West Virginia coal miners in jeopardy. This political treatment of a regulatory question is not going to be affected one whit by the kinds of amendments we are talking about today. It is more likely that dealing with these things issue by issue is going to solve the problem—if it can be solved—of excessive regulatory interference in our lives.

What about the second issue, inflation? Even economists who do not attribute inflation to the expanded money supply admit that the expansion of the money supply enables inflation to take place, whatever the other causes they see as fundamental. But the ability of the government to expand the money supply is not at all affected by any amendments proposed to limit inflation. Furthermore, most theorists who take into account the politics of inflation, as well as the economics of it, recognize that inflation has occurred because governments have made a political choice that inflation under the circumstances is better than the alternatives.

For example, what happens when there is a need for the society to take a sudden decrease in its real income? This occurred in 1974 when there was a terrific increase in oil prices and a large worldwide increase in food prices simultaneously, both brought on by forces beyond the control of any president, whatever the Constitution says, or any Congress, whatever limits were put on it by a constitution. Those price increases created a need to reduce the real incomes of Americans all of a sudden. We could have reduced real incomes but maintained a stable price level by having everyone take a 10–15 percent cut in money wages. But that would have required renegotiating every wage contract and every salary in the society, besides convincing all Americans it was a good idea, and it probably could not have been done.

However, the same real result was accomplished by causing an inflation which, in effect, reduced the real incomes of most Americans simultaneously and very quickly, with the exception of farmers and those who owned oil. This is a case where inflation served a social purpose that probably no other arrangement could have achieved, but we had to do it.

Furthermore, in certain circumstances, inflation has been considered superior to higher unemployment, which could have been achieved by the policies necessary to reduce the rate of inflation. The two-thirds of all American households that own real estate and have borrowed money against it are very great net beneficiaries of inflation. These households are bemoaning their loss of real income through inflationary activity, for which I sympathize with them, but they are not pointing out—except by their behavior in the market—that they are sustaining very large increases in the values of their assets. And these are not fictitious increases or just money illusion increases; they are real because of the operation of leverage debt in times of inflation.

I am not trying to defend long-range inflation as the proper social policy. I am saying that it was adopted and is being continued because our representatives considered it superior at the time to other arrangements. Furthermore, government deficits are not very closely correlated with inflation. In fact, government deficits have been highest in periods of recession. And excess demand, which contributes to inflation, can be generated by the private sector as well as by the public sector.

98

So it is not obvious to me that inflation and the causes of it, and the need to have it under certain circumstances, would be eliminated by any constitutional amendment that prevented government deficits. My conclusion is that neither of the two proximate causes of the dissatisfaction that has led to the debate about whether to adopt constitutional amendments—that is, the expanding role of government in our lives and inflation—would be very effectively removed by these amendments.

Amendments might have some effect, of course. It is likely that reducing the growth of government spending, especially by state and local governments, would reduce the rate of expansion of spending by government, but not necessarily of regulation.

But let us take a larger perspective toward social change for a minute. It is my axiom that all social arrangements are unjust or ineffective to some degree. That is, there is no such thing as a perfect society. Furthermore, I believe that progress consists of a substitution of one set of problems for another, not the elimination of problems; and one can hope that the later set is less intensive than the set replaced. Eric Sevareid once said that all our problems are caused by solutions. That is, the solution to one problem causes a new set of problems, like the new organization to help people stop smoking. It is called "Nicotine Anonymous." A member who has an overwhelming desire to smoke a cigarette calls another member to come over, and they get drunk together. Finally, it is my further belief that all modern societies are so complicated that all actions taken in response to a certain problem lead to unforeseen consequences, which generate other problems that cannot be forecast in advance.

I cite as an example the money market certificate that was adopted in June 1978 to prevent funds from flowing out of savings and loan associations in periods of high short-term interest rates. In terms of that objective, it was an extraordinarily successful invention: it totally prevented the loss of funds by savings and loans during the time when the initial version of it was in effect. As a result, the Federal Reserve lost its power to turn off the housing industry and slow down the economy. Also, the cost of money to savings and loans rose so sharply that some of them became almost financially jeopardized. Thus, the instrument, which was absolutely successful in achieving its stated objective, generated other problems on the side. And I think that is true of all major attempts to deal in policy, whether public or private, in our complicated and interdependent society.

Trial and error is the only way to learn. We have to consider all policies adopted as tentative. We try a policy and see what happens, then modify it as we get feedback from it. It has been said that experience is that wonderful quality that allows us to recognize a mistake when we make it again. We need flexibility of response to cope with the lurching nature of social change as it arises in this kind of world.

Furthermore, it takes time to respond to major social problems. Inflation in America is a relatively recent problem. It started, really, in the late 1960s and has been with us only about ten years. As major problems go, that is not a very long time. We are beginning to decide that we ought to do something about it. Some societies have had worse inflation than ours and have managed to restrain their inflation through public policies. It would be foolish for us to create barriers to learning from, and reacting to, experience, especially when the sources of change come more rapidly than our response time.

It used to be thought that motherhood, apple pie, and the American flag were symbols of consensus and universal approval. But anyone who uses those symbols today is simply not with it, because motherhood jeopardizes the environment, causes too many people, brings up issues of abortion, and so on. Apple pie is fattening and adds to cholesterol, and the American flag has become a symbol of controversy. But one thing we can all agree upon, one thing that is a universal symbol of approbation, is flexibility. Who is in favor of rigidity of response? No one. Everyone favors flexibility. And from the viewpoint of either achieving the desired results regarding inflation and government interference in our lives or allowing the most effective means of responding to social change, I see no net advantage in the amendments that have been proposed.

Discussion

DR. PENNER: Would some of the panelists like to comment on others' talks?

PROFESSOR RIKER: Dr. Downs is quite correct in saying that we usually make decisions issue by issue, but it is exactly this approach that generates the prisoners' dilemmas I was talking about. Unfortunately, I suspect that is the only way we can do it.

On the other hand, Professor Olson speaks of the need for a moral position, in a sense, something deeper than a constitution. But we should not overlook the fact that constitutions are major devices for instructing the population. And one of the things that one can expect from the various self-denying amendments is that they will have an instructive effect. Professor Buchanan was quite right to point out that before the twentieth century, there was a genuine fiscal restraint in the society and that the growth of modern government—all over the world, not only in democracies, but also in dictatorships—represents a loss of that sense of restraint. Without speaking of the merits or demerits of any particular amendment, still, the pursuit of one is in itself an educational device, and we ought not overlook that.

I think Dr. Downs cites the percentage rise of state and local spending incorrectly from the Brookings study. It would be better to look at the proportion of total government expenditures resting in the central government as against the state and local governments. If you go back through the entire history of the country, it turns out that before the Civil War, central government expenditures ran about a fifth to a fourth of the total expenditures by governments. After the Civil War, it went up from a third to two-fifths. After the New Deal, it went up from a half to three-fifths, which is where we stand right now. That seems to me a slightly different picture of the world. The statistic Dr. Downs used is one that shows local governments increasing from a low base, whereas, in fact, the central government has increased from a very high base.

DR. DOWNS: May I say that the expansion of government generally, and especially since the end of World War II, has been much greater in the state and local level than in the federal government. The expansion in general is a response to change in the nature of our society, which renders it quite incomparable with the situation before the Civil War. There were a lot of other arrangements extant at that time that you would not recommend; the fact that something was in existence before the Civil War, it seems to me, is no argument either for or against it. It is irrelevant.

PROFESSOR RIKER: It does say something about Professor Olson's view of the Constitution as something that was made with restraints imposed by the states on federal spending and federal activity. I quite agree that that was the way the Constitution was devised, and I would also insist that the main reason for the mixture of centralism and decentralization that the Constitution embodied was the slavery issue. It was intended, of course, to protect the South and its peculiar institutions.

DR. DOWNS: Are you implying that since we no longer have slavery, we do not need that restraint?

PROFESSOR RIKER: Not at all. I am saying that the main thing that has maintained the federal relationship over the last two hundred years has been the existence of this peculiar institution in the South. And since we have now decided—in the last twenty years or so—that we are not going to allow the South to have that peculiar institution, then it seems to me that the forces making for federalism have substantially disappeared. As a result, we can expect federalism to be a decreasingly significant feature of our society. As blacks become equal citizens, we no longer have a reason for the kind of federalism we had in the past, and so we can't expect federalism to be a particularly significant restraint on federal spending.

PROFESSOR BUCHANAN: As I listen to this exchange, I am reminded of something that my old professor Frank Knight used to say: calling a situation hopeless is equivalent to calling it ideal. I think we are ethically obligated not to take that position, to hope that improvement can take place. That may be blind faith on my part, but it does motivate some of us here.

I would also like to issue an invitation. I would like to invite Professor Olson and Dr. Downs to join me in playing a poker game without rules. The whole notion of the absence of rigidity, the absence of rules, unconstrained flexibility, is absurd. We always operate within rules, and this whole constitutional amendment debate concerns the question of what are the appropriate rules. The debate should center on what I call the constitutional policy questions—what are the rules within which we make pragmatic, program-by-program decisions? As Professor Riker quite properly suggests, we have to consider this problem of rules, the ways in which we constrain ourselves, as a means of getting out of these generalized prisoners' dilemmas.

DR. DOWNS: I must admit I have rarely heard a more distorted interpretation of anything I have said. In the first place, I do not think the situation is hopeless. It is because I have hope that we can work out appropriate responses to existing circumstances within the rules we already have that I do not think we need additional rules.

PROFESSOR BUCHANAN: So, therefore, it is ideal—that is exactly the point.

DR. DOWNS: No, not that the situation is ideal, but that we have the ability to cope with the problems that are facing us. I have hope that we can do that; you are the one who thinks the present arrangements are hopeless. I never said that I was against rules—and I would not want to play poker without rules. What I said was that I did not think that these particular changes in the rules were going to address the issues for which the changes are being suggested. Your idea that we should concentrate only on the constitutional questions and not look at the effects of adopting these amendments is, in my opinion, not only silly, it contradicts what you said in the first place. You pointed out that restraint was part of our past history but we should not argue something on the basis of whether or not it is a restraint; we should worry about the results, and that is my opinion.

We do seem to differ as far as flexibility is concerned. The image I would use for flexibility is a reed which bends in the wind, but which is firmly rooted in one place—the "one place" is the rules that we have already and that have stood us in pretty good stead for a long time. Flexibility does not suggest something that is blowing around like a speck of dust, without any foundation at all, but I do object to your image of something that is completely fixed and does not bend in the wind at any time.

Finally, I think that the whole proposition of adopting these amendments in response to conditions for which they are not really effective answers has some of the flavor of the old story about the singing contest sponsored by the prince. There were two final contestants, and immediately after hearing the first contestant, the prince awarded the prize

103

to the second, without listening to the second contestant, who was in fact even more cacophonous than the first one. That is the kind of risk you are taking.

Can you show me what effect these rules are going to have on the conditions which are giving rise to the desire for them?

PROFESSOR BUCHANAN: You are mixing up two steps in your response to my comment. The first is a question of diagnosis: is the set of existing structures, rules, political process sacrosanct—or is it or is it not ideal? You and Professor Olson implied that we do not want to toy with it.

DR. DOWNS: You are wrongly attributing that to me. I said the question is whether it is effective. I am willing to change the rule if it is effective in achieving what we want to do.

PROFESSOR BUCHANAN: That is mixing up the diagnosis with the second step. That is the point I am making. The first step is diagnosis. The second step is, if you admit that the existing set of rules has somehow failed, say, in the sense Professor Riker talks about, then the debate shifts to consider alternative sets of rules. And I agree with you that it is quite proper, at that point, to talk about predictable outcomes and long-run effects.

DR. DOWNS: Yes, but let's get off this academic plane of talking about abstract principles and talk about expanded government and inflation. Those are the two realities that people are concerned about: what are we going to do about expanded government and inflation?

PROFESSOR BUCHANAN: That would take the whole day, and I do not think there is any point in that. You are using debating tactics now.

PROFESSOR OLSON: I would like to develop a point that I hope will illuminate the exchange we have just heard. Since there are some people here who are not students of political economy or public choice, I will introduce what I like to call the Buchanan-Rawlesian theory of constitutions and morals, familiar as it is to many of us. I am oversimplifying drastically, but a central feature of this theory is the notion that if you have people making decisions about rules—be they constitutional rules or moral rules—in a situation where the impact of these rules on their immediate interests is unclear, this veil of ignorance gives the people making decisions an incentive to choose rules that are, in some sense, efficient or effective, and that, if in operation for a long time, might benefit all the parties to the conclave that agreed upon the rules.

Without for a moment pretending that my statement is even faintly adequate, it seems to me that this line of reasoning contains a large element of truth. This is what underlies my argument that constitutions *do* matter and you *can* improve things sometimes by amending them, but they are not the only thing that matters. A constitutional convention might make a wiser provision for the future than a congress might because of the expectation that a constitutional amendment will last a long time. This provides an incentive for the convention delegates to think, at least in part, about whether the rules will be efficient, will tend to favor all parties over time. This will attenuate a tendency of the parties to seek rules that give them an immediate benefit. In contexts other than a constitutional convention, where we are making judgments that affect our immediate interests, we are less likely to be efficient.

A problem arises because, as ideas change and as pressure groups emerge, this veil of ignorance does not last. Even if we can imagine a constitutional conclave in which the parties behave in an ideal Buchanan-Rawles fashion, it would still be the case that after the constitution was passed and the social and economic and political process had gone on for a while, various parties would see situations where, by amending the constitution or, more important, by reinterpreting the constitution or, more important still, by evading the constitution, they could be made very much better off. As the historical process unfolds and the veil of ignorance lifts, the distinction between constitutional interpretation and evasion on the one hand, and ordinary political squabbling on the other, diminishes. That suggests to me that, while we can do something with constitutional change, we should not assume it will play as big a role as is often supposed in this country.

MR. MARVIN PHAUP, Congressional Budget Office: We have heard a lot about restrictions on social behavior that are not apt to work in the face of incentives and social institutions in conflict with those restrictions. But let us turn the conversation toward some of those restrictions that seem to have been more successful. The First Amendment seems to have been more successful than, say, prohibition. Would anyone comment on why that particular restriction has been more successful?

PROFESSOR RIKER: We have only found it necessary to repeal one constitutional amendment—prohibition. Most of them worked pretty well, even though some of them, the Second Amendment for example, are quite specific and precise amendments. It is indeed the case that constitutional amendments often have the effect of setting a tone to the behavior of people in government. Most of the constitutional amendments, indeed most of the Constitution, involve restrictions not on the general population, but specifically on the actions of government officials. That is precisely what is proposed in the constitutional amendments we are talking about here.

It is true, as Dr. Downs points out, that excessive growth of government is the occasion for this kind of proposal. And there are all sorts of things that such an amendment might attempt to restrict. For example, we provide subsidies for huge numbers of people; we subsidize sugar, cotton, corn, steel, television, textiles, shipping, and so forth. The sum of these subsidies is probably debilitating. An amendment like the ones proposed does not restrict the subsidy getters; it simply restricts the subsidy givers a little bit, just as the First Amendment restricts courts and legislatures, but not people in general.

Consider social security, which ties together a sort of agreement between taxpayers and tax recipients, telling them all that they are going to get something for their money. Yet if we were to separate those two things, not making that sort of deal, I am sure that many people would deeply resent their tax payments but still be glad to have the receipts that the taxes provide. The kind of composite that ties two interests together would be just a little bit more difficult, it seems to me, under a constitutional amendment of this sort. That might be advantageous.

Perhaps the Budget Office can do this. I don't know that it has worked too well, but you probably have different views of that from mine. But it is with that kind of thing that you could expect this amendment to have some practical consequence, on exactly the issues that Dr. Downs raised.

DR. DOWNS: I may not agree with you, but I do think you are talking about the right subject. An amendment might have some restraining effect in some cases. I do not think the costs are worth the benefits, but that is the issue that we should be talking about, I agree.

PROFESSOR OLSON: My view on why the First Amendment has lasted so well while the prohibition amendment was so short-lived is that the First Amendment was consistent with the extraordinary diversity of the United States, whereas the prohibition amendment was inconsistent with that diversity. It tried to impose upon an extremely large and diverse country the morality of what may have been the largest single group in the country but was by no means the whole of the country.

Let us imagine a United States that had been, from the start, 99 percent or more of one religion. I question whether such a United States would ever have passed or, if passed, would have retained a constitutional amendment that really provided all the sorts of freedoms to which we are now accustomed. A large part of the enforcement mechanism for the First Amendment has been that every group, even the largest, has realized it was a minority and that as a minority it gains from restraints that protect it against coalitions of other minorities. The fact that groups could themselves form still other coalitions, perhaps involving some of the people in the preexisting coalitions, was another stabilizing factor. My feeling is that the difference in the fate of these two amendments illustrates the argument I was trying to make earlier today.

PROFESSOR GEOFFREY BRENNAN, Virginia Polytechnic Institute: I would like to offer a comment on one aspect of the discussion so far that strikes me as interesting and worth some attention. The model of "public choice" that seems to have been implicitly agreed to here is one of an electoral process that generates outcomes at variance with the wishes of the electorate.

The disagreement in the debate seems based on another issue—the extent to which political agents, even if not limited by the political process, might behave with moral constraint. On the one hand, Downs and Olson apparently believe that though majoritarian processes do not work too well, we nevertheless ought not to apply additional constraints because this only makes things harder for the politicians and their advisers as they seek to do the "right thing." Indeed, as I understand Professor Olson's position, additional constraints (including, specifically, balanced budget restrictions) are totally ineffective: there is no point in mending the fence at one point if the cows will simply stray out through a hole somewhere else. On this account, only moral constraints *can* work.

Professors Buchanan and Riker seem to be more skeptical about the effectiveness of purely internal moral considerations in constraining the behavior of politicians, but also more hopeful concerning the possibilities of institutional reform. In their view, the only possibility for improvement lies in changing the rules under which politicians operate.

Wherever one stands on these matters, it seems to me to be worth noting explicitly both the nature of disagreement and the prior consensus. If we can agree that political processes are currently failing in some way, then this in itself is an important step, even if the matter of what we ought to do about it remains debatable.

DR. DOWNS: Certainly, there are problems with the existing system, because all systems have problems. As I said, it is my axiom that all social arrangements, all societies, contain significant degrees of injustice and there is no way to eliminate all injustice. You may disagree with that, but if you accept that proposition, then the question is which form of injustice do you prefer? It is not whether you want to compare the present form of injustice with some perfect absence of it. And I certainly do not dispute in principle the possibility that a constitutional amendment might be a good idea to deal with some problem, but I do dispute that this particular type of amendment is going to deal with the particular causes for which it has been suggested. That is my argument.

PROFESSOR OLSON: I would like to respond to Professor Brennan's point also, because it is quite fundamental, and I sense that I have failed to state properly a basic element of my own argument.

Let us look for a moment, just as an example, at tax loopholes and subsidies to small groups, say, sugar beet or sugar cane growers. (By "small," I mean small in relationship to the whole of society.) Our society definitely has a problem: it passes too many tax loopholes, thereby raising the tax burden on the income not subject to loopholes. I also see a serious problem in that many special subsidies make no sense, either in terms of any desire for a more egalitarian distribution of income, or from an efficiency point of view. On balance, they tend to be inefficient.

Now, let us perform the mental experiment of changing the Constitution to require a two-thirds vote in committees or on the floor of Congress for tax loopholes, somehow defined, and for subsidies to special groups, somehow defined. That measure would be fine with me and it might help a little. But I suspect it would not change things a lot.

Why wouldn't it change things a lot? We know that if there had been a referendum on a tax loophole for this or that big company, any tax loophole that had as its beneficiaries a tiny subset of the electorate, would not pass—or if it did, it would be because of some massive inequality in the campaign funds available to the two sides. Similarly, subsidies for special groups will not, on the whole, pass a majoritarian standard. So how do these features come into our legislation? There are two main causes: one, the organized lobbies that support particular interests; and two, the fact that the individual citizen has no incentive to get information about public affairs, including the public affairs of subsidies and tax loopholes; that is to say, the individual citizen finds information about public goods a public good itself. A typical citizen has a 1 in 50 million or 10 million chance that his or her vote will change the outcome of an election. It would not be rational for a typical citizen to get a lot of information about public affairs—what goes on in these congressional committees is watched by a few lobbies but not by the mass of the people.

Although it is true that requiring two-thirds instead of a simple majority would have some effect, the requirement would not, by and large, deal with the fundamental problem. That fundamental problem is the asymmetry in influence between organized pressure groups and an electorate composed of individuals, each of whom has little incentive to study special interest measures or to work to defeat them.

I am not arguing that morality can always be relied on. If, as I argued, constitutional inhibitions are a scarce resource, then moral inhibitions are even more so! You may recall the delightful passage from Thurber in which one woman asks another, "Why didn't they repeal inhibition while they were at it?" There are strong moral inhibitions, but also widespread desires to escape or evade them. So I certainly would not want to be misunderstood as saying that inhibition will always do the trick. The argument is that the electoral rules, though a part of the problem, in fact the constitutional part of the problem, are very far indeed from being the whole problem. Other factors, like the power of pressure groups, the degree of diversity of the society, the coalitions which are expedient given the particular configuration of interests—they are what matters most, and they would not be changed much by a balanced budget amendment.

PATTY PRADO, Bank of America of San Francisco: I have more of a comment than a question. Being from California, I have learned that these issues cannot be dealt with in terms of abstractions and theories. Proposition 13 and its effects, and those of the state and local spending limitation proposal which has qualified for the ballot in California, are issues our institution has put a lot of work into understanding, but we also get stuck at just the point that Mr. Downs raised: Who would benefit from these proposals; who would lose; what are these benefits and these losses; and what are the effects on inflation, regulation, private investment, and economic growth? I would like to suggest that these issues be specifically addressed somewhere in this discussion.

SPENCER REIBMAN, Office of Congressman John Rousselot: Dr. Downs seems to assume cavalierly that if we had no inflation, we would not have this call for a constitutional amendment. Granted, without inflation, people would not be pushed into higher tax brackets, and that part of the problem would evaporate, but there is still reason to change the rules by which we increase tax rates.

Clearly, if we had no inflation and the rate of growth of federal spending were equal to real economic growth, then in a situation where special groups or citizens in general want more spending, there would still be pressure to raise revenues somehow through higher taxes.

So the real question is whether it is possible to change the rules of the game on taxation. The power to tax is insidious because it can be so alluring, yet so destructive. Congress does not follow a set of standard financial rules as any major corporation would in the sense that Congress does not estimate the discounted present value of its tax and spending policies. Instead, it establishes spending targets, then raises taxes without regard to the negative effects higher tax rates will have on the economy.

So an argument can be made for some sort of a constitutional amendment that is based on financial principles and that recognizes that the power to tax can be destructive. Yes, we would still have regulatory problems, but at least we would put a dent in the major problem—the power to tax.

DR. DOWNS: You don't mean the power; you mean its being used in ways you do not agree with.

MR. REIBMAN: That's right. The power is being used in ways with which many of us do not agree. This is why we are asking for curbs on the power to raise tax rates.

DR. DOWNS: There are two problems to which I think the amendments are responding: inflation and the expanded role of government. Federal income tax rates have not, by and large, put people into higher and higher tax brackets over time, because Congress has reduced tax rates as inflation has increased.

MR. REIBMAN: That is not exactly correct.

DR. DOWNS: The fraction of personal income going into federal income taxes has not risen very substantially in the last few years, in spite of inflation. If you disagree, there is no point in arguing further here unless we see what the facts are. If you are asking whether an amendment would reduce taxation or reduce the role of government, that is the right thing to discuss, I agree, but I do not think that government interference in our lives would be substantially reduced by an amendment. Are you talking about a balanced budget amendment or a limitation on spending?

MR. REIBMAN: A balanced budget amendment requiring that to raise tax rates, you need some super majority.

DR. DOWNS: I think that the interference in our lives today is not primarily caused by government spending or by the level of taxation. It is caused by regulations, by the increasing interference with all kinds of things we do, by having to fill out government forms, get permissions, and things of that nature. These things are not responsive to or related to the amount of government spending. The problem you are addressing is that people do not like taxation; and what you are proposing might well limit or slow down the growth of government as a fraction of GNP, although that growth has not been staggering. But I do not think your proposal addresses itself to the real causes of people's resentment against government, which are, first, the expansion of state and local government and, second, the expansion of regulatory interference in our lives.

Your suggestion might even aggravate the problem by causing a government agency that cannot finance research activities of its own to pass the burden of proof on to you because you have the funds to do it. That is what some of the regulatory agencies are doing now. Rather than finding out whether, say, an air pollution regulation will really affect health, they just adopt it because they do not have enough funds or they do not have the time or Congress has not given them the power to investigate the real relationship between that regulation and health. They leave it up to you, as a private firm, to cope with this, to prove one way or the other whether their assumption is true.

MR. REIBMAN: Perhaps, then, new regulations should be interpreted to be synonymous with taxes? Perhaps they too should require a super majority?

DR. DOWNS: That is impossible; it would be a distortion of the language. It would require some different kind of amendment to restrict the government's power of regulation. That is not what we are considering now.

DR. PENNER: Professor Buchanan, you made an intriguing comment when you suggested that your work with Geoff Brennan was leading to the conclusion that perhaps it would be most effective not to set a spending limit or require a balanced budget limit, but rather to limit the tax base that the government can use. Do you mean limit it to a certain kind of income or certain kinds of sales or what?

PROFESSOR BUCHANAN: I threw that in because it has not entered into any of these particular proposals for a constitutional amendment, but it does seem to us that it has certain advantages over the others. You simply allow governments only certain specific bases of taxation, and people always have the option to reduce taxes by not utilizing that particular base, not earning that particular type of income, or not spend-

111

ing on that particular type of commodity. It allows for flexibility in response . . .

DR. DOWNS: Yay!

PROFESSOR BUCHANAN: . . . a great deal of flexibility, but contained within certain predictable rules. Obviously, I cannot go through the analysis here, but I mentioned it because it is one thing that is not present in any of the current alternatives.

PROFESSOR ATTIAT OTT, Clark University: Dr. Downs, your use of the phrase "had to do it" to describe the government's inflation decision bothered me. The government had choices—to trade off inflation against unemployment or capital formation. Your implication that we "had to do it" contradicts your belief in trial and error.

DR. DOWNS: No, I said the time we had to do it was in response to the food price increase and the oil price increase.

PROFESSOR OTT: But we could have done something else altogether.

DR. DOWNS: What? What would you have done?

PROFESSOR OTT: I would have opted for unemployment instead, but I would not have said I "have to do" it—I would not know. See, we learn from trial and error. I would say now the effect of inflation, as the administration has found out, is much worse, and perhaps they should have let unemployment take its course. I do not believe you have to do anything without looking at alternatives, and the electorate has to have something to do with the choice, given that we are supposed to be a democratic society.

Another comment is that if you believe, as Professor Riker said, that a motion can be passed that is against the self-interest of the people, then anything you do, whether you are fighting inflation or fighting unemployment, could also be against our own self-interest. How do you deal with that?

DR. DOWNS: It's simple—I don't believe it.

PROFESSOR OTT: You don't agree? That's not good enough.

DR. DOWNS: It is apparently good enough for you. You accept it because he believes it; why don't you accept that I do not believe it?

PROFESSOR OTT: How do you reconcile his position and yours?

DR. DOWNS: It's easy: he is wrong and I am right.

PROFESSOR RIKER: It is true; it is a mathematical fact.

DR. DOWNS: Didn't you learn from coming to Washington that facts are negotiable?

PROFESSOR RIKER: I know, that is why we have Pareto pessimal results.

PETER FURTH, Louis Furth, Inc.: I have heard from the panel two sorts of diagnoses of problems. One is the ills of inflation, growth of government, regulation, and that sort of thing. But perhaps these things are just reflections or symptoms of the greater underlying problem that Professors Riker and Olson talked about earlier: that is, the system we have. No matter what we do about these present-day problems, those underlying forces will still be there and will give us new problems in the future. Maybe they will be different; maybe they will be the same.

If you take that view, the prescription of a balanced budget or spending limit or any other amendment to the Constitution will not, as Dr. Downs said, cure the problem. It will only make us believe we have done something about the problem. Maybe we are attacking it the wrong way, then.

That takes us to the question of whether the problem is cancerous. Is it going to kill us in the long run as a country? Is it something worth seeing to today, or should we just leave it alone—like a stomachache that hurts but is not going to kill us?

PROFESSOR OLSON: My feeling is that the balanced budget amendment has been oversold as a panacea. I am cautious about panaceas, including my own recommendations. A large part of our problem is the accumulation over time of increasingly powerful lobbies representing small segments of the society. These lobbies pressure for various types of government intervention, tax loopholes, and other things, which are bad for efficiency but which serve the interest of each of these groups taken separately.

What kind of a cure could there be for this? Changing the Constitution is something one might consider, and I certainly do not rule it out. I am very much an admirer of the Buchanan-type reasoning about constitutions, which is applicable here and can perhaps be part of a solution. But an even more important part of the answer would be

113

efforts to undercut, through more liberal and cosmopolitan policies, the power of the cartels and lobbies we are accumulating.

Let us take for an example one of the most venerable recommendations in all of economics, free trade. Free trade will help us a great deal because it will ensure that any cartel, or indeed any industry with a strong union, in this country, if it deals in a product that is traded internationally, will be greatly constrained by foreign producers. Because foreign producers are far away and speak a different language and so on, they would be hard to organize in the same cartel or the same union. So I think a part of the solution is freer trade.

Another part would be free hospitality to capital movements, including multinational firms. We do better than most countries in this, but we could do better still. Foreign companies could come in and undercut cartels in this country. Also, if we are doing something stupidly because some lobby has won particular legislation that reduces social efficiency, then that will change our competitive advantage. Foreign countries will adjust to the situation, and the new pattern of trade that results, though it will not be perfectly efficient, will at least limit the extent of the social loss.

Another thing that helps is free migration of labor. If I am right in thinking one of the reasons we have had, say, freedom of speech and freedom of religion in this country is that we were so diverse, then relatively liberal immigration policies will not only have the benefit of maintaining our diminishing heterogeneity but also undercut various cartelistic arrangements. So some part of the problem—only part, I admit—can be solved by the traditional liberal methods of free trade and free factor mobility.

PROFESSOR RIKER: I agree thoroughly. But the constitutional approach would help very much to cure exactly the problems that you mentioned. It is true that the problems we are talking about are inherent in majority voting; there is no question of that. But it is also true that if you start from any given position, status quo, and if the policy space has more than one dimension, then it is possible to construct a path such that you can get from the status quo to any point in the space. . . .

DR. DOWNS: It is theoretically possible, but I live in a different world from the world you talk about.

PROFESSOR RIKER: . . . and what you can do then is slow down the process, place constraints on the process, of going to some point that is desired by a very small number of people. That is exactly what constitutional constraints have always been. The new proposals are just another constitutional restraint to make it more difficult for us to do things that we probably do not regard as desirable anyway. That is exactly what the separation of powers is supposed to do; it is exactly what federalism is supposed to do. An amendment is just another element of control over the extreme possibilities that are open to us under majority rule. I do not see why one should be so upset about it.

PROFESSOR BUCHANAN: We have been talking here about alternative constitutional rules to impose some limits on the power of government to tax and to spend. We have disagreed about them, but still we have spent two days considering them. This could not have happened at the American Enterprise Institute three years ago. That it happened now is a sign of the strength of the popular movement behind these alternatives.

Part Four

A Roundup of the Policy Issues Raised by Proposals for Constitutional Limits

Introduction

Robert P. Griffin, Chairman

Aside from earthquakes, the plague, and a few other types of major disasters, the last thing that members of Congress are likely to welcome to town is a constitutional convention to consider a balanced budget amendment, regardless of their individual views on the merits of such a proposal.

Of course, members of Congress have the standard concerns that a convention might roam beyond the subject of fiscal responsibility. But I rather think there are other worries on Capitol Hill as well. For example, such a historic convention could push Congress and the White House out of the television news and off the front page of every newspaper in the country. Is it also possible that a convention might bring new political figures to national attention—some Senate and presidential candidates, perhaps?

Our focus here is the likely political impact of the current drive for a balanced budget amendment, whether it succeeds or falls short. What will it do to the race for president and the races for congressional seats? Just what will Congress really do if and when the number of petitioning states reaches, if it should, the magic number thirty-four? Oh yes, Article V says that Congress *shall* call a convention, but just how will Congress react? These are only some of the subjects of this discussion. In the course of it, we will no doubt find other intriguing political questions raised by the current effort to amend the Constitution.

Politics and Economics of a
Balanced Budget Amendment

Charles L. Schultze

Under the economic circumstances that now face the country, I believe it is essential, as a matter of public policy, that the federal budget deficit be steadily reduced and the budget be moved into balance. A balanced budget is proper policy for today's economy, but that is no warrant for enshrining it for all times in the Constitution as the fundamental law of the land. That would be roughly equivalent to having frozen into the Constitution the free coinage of silver, the charter of the First National Bank, the Sherman Antitrust Act, and, Lord help us, the Interstate Commerce Commission, each of which was seen in its time as an answer to a particular set of very pressing economic problems. I will address the economics of a proposed amendment later on, but first let me speak to the politics of it, in the broadest sense of that term.

In my judgment the requirement would be impossible to administer. Every January the president must submit a budget for a fiscal year ending twenty months later. Obviously, the expected balance in the budget will depend upon the forecast of the course of the economy over that twenty months, and, since we have never been very successful in forecasting recessions before they occur, revenues at times are going to be substantially different from what we expect. All sorts of other things change, too, with changes in economic conditions—expenditures for Medicare, Medicaid, unemployment insurance, and other entitlement programs.

Thus, if we meant literally to balance the budget, we would spend the year continually revising taxes in order to balance them with expenditures. And, since the time lags make it impossible to do this balancing with any frequency with any success, we would end up having to budget a large surplus. If we really meant to balance the budget, we would have to advance a large surplus to handle the not unlikely contingency that our economic forecast would turn out to be wrong. Now, it may turn out that we are not really serious; but if we are, then the proposal is not for a balanced budget but for a surplus.

Another political issue is just what are we going to balance? What do we mean by revenues and what do we mean by expenditures? What is in the budget is not fixed. Currently, there are a number of federal loan programs that are not included in the budget; they are not defined as federal expenditures and do not count in the deficit. Up until 1968, the trust funds were not in the budget. An amendment to the Constitution is something we at least hope will last not five or ten years, but hundreds of years. And over time, the temptation would grow to move more and more expenditures off the budget and make them into so-called off-budget items in order to meet a balanced budget requirement.

So what do you mean by a balanced budget? What revenues and what expenditures? Imagine the Founding Fathers in 1789 trying to write a balanced budget provision.

I can see twenty pages of accounting definitions in the Constitution, and even that would not be enough. No definition could cover all the kinds of circumstances that arise, and I think it would become routine for accounting matters to be challenged in the courts. Someone might suggest that we write a broad amendment and let Congress handle it with laws. With that approach, I assure you as an ex-budget director, you will get budget balance by accounting ingenuity. But if you write a lot of accounting specifications into the Constitution, then you probably open the matter up to significant judicial interpretation. In fact, judicial interpretation would not be limited to the accounting conventions of the budget, but it would gradually tend to expand over a large number of important aspects of budgetary and economic policy making as well.

Let us look closely at one proposed amendment to limit federal spending. It is not a balanced budget amendment; it is the Friedman-McCracken amendment of the National Tax Limitation Committee, which dealt carefully with the problem from a technical standpoint. They faced up to the enforcement problem, and proposed in their amendment that any congressman or group of congressmen could sue the treasurer—not the secretary of the Treasury, but the treasurer of the United States—in the U.S. District Court for the District of Columbia to enforce the provision. This could obviously result in frequent lawsuits over budget policy.

The amendment further provides that the treasurer of the United States shall "have the authority over outlays by any unit or agency of the Government of the United States when required by a court order enforcing the provisions of the Article." The drafters correctly recognized that a court-ordered expenditure cutback could not be enforced by requiring 535 senators and congressmen to agree on what programs to cut and by how much. Hence, they were forced to transfer authority over budget programs, first, from the Congress to the courts with respect to the size of the total cut, and second, from the Congress to a single

121

person in the executive branch with respect to the allocation of the cuts. The sensible budget process established by the Congressional Budget Act of 1974 would be completely short-circuited.

Enforcing a balanced budget amendment would require a similar approach. The decision whether to balance the budget would have to be lodged either in the courts or, subject to a court order, in the executive. And, when a court order requires that the budget be balanced, the court itself or an executive official would have to decide whether to do so through tax increases or expenditure cuts, and what specific taxes to increase or expenditures to cut.

The 200-year-old structure of the Constitution which distributes authority over taxes and expenditures between Congress and the executive would be radically altered, and substantial new powers would be granted to the courts. The courts would be determining tax and spending policy as they interpret the application of the amendment's language to myriad unforeseen circumstances over the next century. We are, I presume, talking about something that is written for the century.

Let us look at the incentives for bad government under such an amendment. Faced with particular national needs, especially in periods of recession and declining revenues, congresses and presidents would be sorely tempted to engage in very harmful, wasteful, and inefficient practices as a means of avoiding constraints imposed by the amendment. Human nature is human nature, and we are dealing with a long period of time. For example, federal unemployment insurance payments rise sharply in times of recession, just when revenues are falling and when following an annually balanced budget constraint would really pinch. To avoid having these expenditures in the budget, why not simply devise a new set of regulations over private industry that require business firms to pay any laid-off worker his or her full wages for, say, up to a year or some other period of time? Federal unemployment insurance payments would be removed from the budget, unemployment compensation would be taken care of, and, of course, any flexibility in the economy would be wrecked.

Take another example. Many federal expenditures are grant-in-aid programs that help state and local governments meet certain federally mandated requirements where national or regional interests are at stake. Municipal waste treatment plants are such a case. An obvious way to help balance the federal budget would be to keep the federal requirements but make the states and localities pay the full cost. Just shift the burden more and more over to the states and localities for pollution control, Medicaid, welfare, and so on. Wherever the federal government makes grants for investment purposes, it would be tempting to replace them with guaranteed loans, which involve no budget outlay, or with

122

an interest subsidy, which has small immediate budget outlay that cumulates over time.

The federal government would have a major interest in finding taxes that do not decline sharply in recession. Again, remember we are dealing with a long period of time for pressures to accumulate. A federal tax on wealth or property is an obvious candidate, because wealth and property values do not fluctuate as sharply as does income. This tax would be tempting to the federal government despite the difficulties it would create for state and local tax bases and what it would mean for federal tax policy to have such a base.

In other words, mandating an annually balanced federal budget in the Constitution would set in motion some major forces that, over a span of years, would change the economic, social, and tax policies of the federal government in very fundamental ways, virtually all of which would, I think, impose onerous burdens on business firms, state and local governments, and individual citizens.

Let me speak, finally, to the economic impact of such a requirement during periods of recession. Obviously, balancing a budget depends not only on expenditure programs or tax rates, but also on the level of income in the economy. When output, employment, and income decline, then necessarily, if we are going to have a balanced budget, we must either slash expenditures or raise tax rates. But, of course, it is not enough simply to cut expenditures by the amount of the prospective deficit, or to raise tax rates by enough to recover the amount of the projected deficit, because that action itself would drive the economy down further. And so, if it looks as if we will have a $20 billion deficit to cover, recession conditions mean that we will need to cut expenditures or raise taxes by a lot more than $20 billion to do so.

Let us take a look at the magnitudes that would have been involved in 1974–1975. In fiscal 1974, the federal budget was almost in balance; there would have been a $4.5 billion deficit. Then we had a major recession: the unemployment rate rose to 9 percent, GNP fell by 2.5 percent, and in 1976 the federal budget deficit was up to $66 billion. It would not have been enough to slash $66 billion out of expenditures or add $66 billion to taxes—that would have driven the economy down further. Plans would need to be made for more than that. We used three econometric models to see how much of an expenditure cut would have been needed. The models gave different results, but they were in a fairly close range. It turns out that expenditures would have had to be cut by about $50 billion in 1975 and $100 billion in 1976 in order, ultimately, to get a balanced budget. The unemployment rate would have been about 12 percent, GNP would have fallen not by 2 percent but by near 10 or 11 percent, and we would have had the first true, full-

123

fledged, major depression since the 1920s. Thus, the consequences of trying to have an annually balanced budget can turn out to be horrendous.

But quite apart from this economic point, a balanced budget amendment would set in motion things that nobody really understands or fully appreciates. Tremendous pressures would be generated by enshrining this sort of thing in the Constitution. They would lead to major change and, I think, generally to deleterious change in the whole structure of government and in the relationship of the federal government to state and local governments and to industry.

Problems and Prospects of Budget Balance

Richard G. Lugar

I would like to begin by raising the general question, Why is there so much interest in this subject? One reason is that the people of America, in large numbers, are deeply concerned about inflation, not as a temporary phenomenon, but as one in which the peaks of inflation appear to many to be veering out of control. We may escape a disastrous situation this time around; in fact, if the economy is cooling off, conceivably inflation will do so, too. Those who come to testify before Congress suggest, however, that there is a residual floor of 6, 7, or 8 percent inflation which is stuck in the economy, and that during unhappy periods, we will have gusts in the double digits or perhaps worse.

Some argue that this is a short-term phenomenon, that this type of inflation has not characterized most of the twentieth century, and that it is a post–Vietnam war phenomenon. If, indeed, inflation is not that much of a problem for the American people, then I suspect the balanced budget amendment idea will eventually dissipate and fail. A majority of businesses, individuals, and institutions will have groused about inflation, but will have come to cope with it and, in their own ways, will simply have indexed themselves sufficiently or put sufficient insulation around themselves to learn to live with it.

But there are a good many people, and I am one of them, who suspect that there is reason for deep concern about federal spending and inflation. The reason we talk about a balanced budget amendment is that some of us have come to believe that there is a structural flaw in the way Congress approaches taxing, spending, and budgetary policies. The founders may have anticipated this structural flaw, but perhaps not the virulence of it that many of us experience in a practical way. Pressures for spending are intense; they come in the form of not only special interest groups, but also very special people that come into our lives and make appeals for compassionate expenditures. Resistance to expenditure is very diffuse. As a result, we have a structural imbalance in the budgetary process each year.

I think that everyone who has served in the House or the Senate feels this imbalance. Of course, we can react to it in different ways. We

125

may tell the nurses who come and want further training and expansion of their program that, in the overall interest of the nation, they simply will have to be satisfied with what they are receiving now—or perhaps suffer a 25 percent cutback. But we do this ultimately at our peril as elected officials because the problem is compounded by 250 other well-deserving groups. The gist of American politics is, in essence, accommodation of all these persons; worse still, it is accommodation plus indexing. We could have given every group in our society a 3 percent increase in expenditures over last year's budget and still have balanced the budget this year. We did not attempt to do that. Essentially, we are attempting to give each group 7 or 8 percent to hold them whole, and failure to add 7 or 8 percent to each and every group has come under attack for cutting the group in real terms, even if not in absolute terms.

Now, we are not completely evenhanded in this respect. For example, in the Senate Foreign Relations Committee, we have cut foreign aid, even in absolute terms. Why? Because the committee read the tea leaves and decided the constituency for foreign aid is not so good, and therefore we do not have to hold foreign aid recipients whole. But on the other hand, there is the case of food stamps. The food stamp program still has a ceiling of $6.2 billion on fiscal 1980 expenditures. Why? Because when the Agriculture Committee considered food stamps in the 1977 act, we anticipated that, given the astronomical leaps and bounds of expenditures under that program, we ought to put a limit on it. We did so by legislation, and the cap is still there. Now, this year, the administration comes and points out that $6.2 billion will not do, and that $6.9 billion will be required. As I recall, OMB said $7.2 billion and the Congressional Budget Office estimated $7.5 billion; the Senate voted $6.9 billion, and the House split the difference at $7.2 billion. But some are now suggesting that there ought to be no cap at all, or at least no meaningful cap, on the food stamp program; that Congress ought simply to supply the money needed to cover everyone who is entitled to benefits. Many programs have the characteristics of food stamps. If the basic philosophy is that Congress's work is simply to add up the best estimate of what these programs cost, then one begins to add. Whatever is in the budget resolutions may be quite beside the point.

This is our dilemma, and we can each decide how serious we think it is. Some think it is not serious at all; indeed, some favor completely the kind of redistribution that occurs in these kinds of programs and would like to see them expanded. These people realize that a balanced budget requirement would jeopardize entitlement programs and programs that are indexed to inflation. My analysis at this point is that many of the senators who are deeply concerned about inflation and about controlling spending favor a constitutional amendment and are attempting to agree on a specific proposal. Those who are not all that concerned about balancing budgets, but see as the major role of Congress the fulfillment of American dreams in social programs, are going to oppose such an amendment.

Charles Schultze has argued that it is awfully hard to define terms like expenditures, balance, and revenues. Indeed it is. The accounting problems are prodigious and my guess is that that will continue to be the case. It is very difficult to forecast the future and to estimate revenues in advance. This is why it seems to me that, in approaching a budget balancing amendment, one must have a certain degree of caution and a great deal of flexibility.

The particular amendment that I have suggested simply says that we cannot adopt an unbalanced budget unless we have a two-thirds majority of both houses. That does not escape all the technical criticisms that have been made already, including that of the difficulty of achieving perfect balance. We presently estimate both expenditures and revenues, and I am willing to concede that there is no way to project perfect balance down to the last dollar. Nor do I want to go into courts of law on each and every issue of minor imbalance or accounting strategies. What I want is a presumption—a presumption that the *goal* is balance. That is not the presumption now. The current presumption is not even close to that, as a matter of fact. There is no attempt being made, as we discuss the budget this year, to say that our goal is balance; our goal is to come somewhere between $20 billion to $30 billion in deficit. I am saying our goal, our presumption, has to be balance. If there are overriding considerations of national catastrophe, economics, or national security, imbalance is permissible. It is not quite so easy to get an extraordinary majority of two-thirds to conclude that deficits are necessary, and this will help to ensure the presumption of balance.

This is not a satisfying amendment to those who are looking for rigorous expenditure limits tied to GNP or to some other specified number. I am inclined to feel that that kind of proposal is likely to be frustrated by its very specificity. I think, too, that it may be unwise to adopt specific numerical limits. We may, for example, need to develop for our defense—quite apart from the SALT issue—things like the mobile missile and the cruise missile. These are expensive undertakings. I am not sure we can accomplish all this within precise expenditure limits. It may well be necessary for our defense to raise taxes, if need be, to pay for things that are absolutely vital. I would like to leave that option open, as I think it is under a flexible balanced budget amendment.

It seems to me that we finally have to achieve some consensus about whether the American people want to move toward greater fiscal restraint and balance, or whether they do not. At this point, there appears to be a substantial majority of people in the country who want Congress to control itself. This number is much greater than the number who have lost all hope of this, and therefore would suggest that a constitutional convention come into being to control Congress. I think that the more responsible course would be serious consideration by the Judiciary Committees of the Senate and House of all of the issues we are discussing today, a careful crafting of constitutional language, and then the proposal of a balanced budget amendment.

Instead, what we have in the Senate Judiciary Committee, for example, is perhaps one hearing every month in which a couple of senators say their piece. This is an obvious stalling effort in which Senate liberals simply hope the whole issue will go away like a bad dream—that somehow, having reached its crest, the issue will disappear into the dark. Their hope is that we will forget this foolishness about budget balancing and fiscal control and soon return to what liberals see as the agenda for the country.

My guess is that the issue will not go away. Next year the problem will be more intense than this year. There will be public pressures, therefore, for activity. I would hope so. And I would suggest, therefore, that our forum today concentrate on those things that ought to be involved in the continuing discussion. I believe the public wants balance, but I also believe that the public is highly ambivalent on the whole issue. The findings of the Everett Ladd article in *Fortune* (December 18, 1978) are that the public overall, by 82 percent, thinks the federal government spends too much. But the public also wants expenditures for many things, with maybe only foreign aid and "welfare" as areas where severe cuts would be tolerated. We are going to have to balance those issues.

The Balanced Budget:
A View from the Congress

David R. Obey

Senator Lugar indicated that there are those who place other values above fiscal stability. There may be, but frankly, I know very few, and I certainly do not count myself among that group because I think almost any rational person will recognize that without fiscal stability, we cannot have social stability; and if we do not have either fiscal stability or social stability, we certainly do not have political stability.

Charles Schultze has listed the usual reasons for opposing the concept of balanced budget locked into the Constitution, but let me summarize some of the problems again, as I see them. First: economically, it makes no sense. Any idiot would want to move toward a balanced budget given the economic situation we have today and the inflationary pressures today and, I submit, the high level of employment we have today. But I would think that we would also grant that in some years, a balanced budget would, as Charles Schultze pointed out, turn a recession into a depression, or turn a small recession into a large one, and I do not consider that economic stability or fiscal stability. But that is what would happen, in my judgment, unless the constitutional limitation were shot through with so many exceptions as to be almost meaningless. But, in fact, this discussion usually reminds me of one of the old spelling rules we used to have. When I went to grade school, we had the old rule: "*i* before *e,* except after *c* or when sounded like *a,* as in neighbor or weigh." And you can go on and on with exceptions if you want, and I think we would have to if we were to fashion a constitutionally mandated limitation.

The second problem reminds me of the old song, "Anything You Can Do I Can Do Better." I have great faith in the ability of any legislative body, state or federal, to find ingenious ways around any limit we could draft and put into the Constitution. Does anybody here really think that Charles Schultze or Charls Walker or Russell Long could not invent whatever bookkeeping system is needed to get around an amendment? For every clever device that we establish in print, we can find a clever legislator or clever somebody else to get around it. In my judgment, budget accounting gimmicks would change under this system as fast as football defenses, and that has been pretty fast the last few years.

Third, on a more philosophical plane, I again would agree with Charles Schultze. I believe that we ought to protect the Constitution from the orthodoxy of the moment. I operate on the principle that tomorrow can be more screwed up than today, and if you use precedents, it usually will be. The unfortunate fact of life is that politics is imitative. George McGovern had his mailing list back in 1968; today Richard Viguerie has his. I do not think that is an improvement in the welfare of the country. If conservatives could lock into the Constitution the economic doctrine of a balanced budget in a time of inflation, is that not a precedent for other groups to try, in periods of high unemployment, to lock into the Constitution the doctrine of government as the employer of last resort? Are we not better off if we remember that the Constitution really defines process? It defines a way of doing things. It defines the pattern and the limits of government. It does not define the product of government. To the extent we start cluttering up the Constitution with things like this, we move away from what I think is the proper view of the Constitution.

On a more practical level, what if Congress does pass a balanced budget but the laws of economics do not cooperate? What if all members of Congress convert suddenly—in one striking moment, à la St. Paul—to Laffer economics, and we proceed to cut taxes by the precise amount recommended to us by Jack Kemp, but the economy misses the curve? What do we do in that instance? Do we shoot Jack Kemp? I do not know.

On an even more practical level, is it really in the national interest to require extreme adjustments in federal program levels in order to accommodate the wide fluctuations we will inevitably have in the economy, or to be prepared to raise tax rates as an alternative? What are the programmatic implications of that? What happens to services that government provides to business, to workers, to travelers, to consumers, to local governments, you name it, ad nauseam, if the budget for these services must move in unison with economic changes?

I recently went through that exercise on the House floor, partly to learn for myself what it would mean and partly to illustrate to the House what it would mean. There was an article recently which indicated that Marriner Eccles, a number of years ago, decided that the way to deal with this question, in his time, was simply to propose that the Congress immediately adopt a balanced budget for the current year rather than in some distant year. What I tried to do in a small way was the same thing. We drafted a budget that tried to balance the budget this year, not just in aggregate terms, but right down to the program-by-program level. I tried to do it in a neutral way, leaving aside my own program biases, recognizing that Congress is never going to balance the budget only by gouging the Pentagon or only by gouging the social programs (the political balance in that place would not allow that). I also tried to recognize the facts of life as far as various programs are concerned, the government's contractual obligations, and how different programs work.

I followed three principles. One is that the budget ought to be balanced totally through spending reductions, because I think that is what the public really thinks of when they hear us talking about a balanced budget. Second, I assumed that payments to individuals under programs like social security and veterans' pensions would really not be cut to any great degree. Third, I tried to make cuts in all programs, recognizing that Congress would not be able to gouge only Molly's cow; they would have to gouge everybody's.

The first problem you run into in that kind of exercise is, as Charles Schultze has indicated, that when you cut budgets, people lose jobs. Government workers begin to lose jobs, employees of companies who have government contracts begin to lose jobs, and it ripples throughout the economy. We were told by the Congressional Budget Office (CBO) that if we wanted to balance the budget by eliminating the $25 billion deficit that was in the House budget resolution, we would really have to cut about $38 billion.

As you know, the budget is divided into five parts. Interest is one, and we cannot really do much to affect what we pay out in interest. A second is payments to individuals, estimated in the budget this year at about $205–209 billion. Excluding those two items leaves approximately $277–280 billion in the other three budget categories. Thirty percent of that, about $82 billion, would go for payments to states; 47 percent would go for defense and international affairs; and 23 percent would go for federally run domestic programs.

As I said, there is nothing we can do about interest. In the second category, payments to individuals, I do not think Congress would make much of a cut, but we judged that we might save $6 billion if we capped social security increases this year at 7 percent rather than allowing the full increase to go into effect—and if we reduced individual entitlements under the food stamp program from the presently mandated 100 percent of minimum nutritional requirement to 80 percent of the minimum nutritional requirement daily, and if we reduced maximum unemployment benefits under unemployment compensation, and so on. If we did things like that, we might get as much as $6 billion out of that item, but I do not think Congress would go very much deeper.

In the area of grants to states, we could save, we thought, about

$9.5 billion if we wanted to, among other things, cut AFDC, which is a very unpopular program, in half, which would reduce benefits by $27 per month for each child; if we wanted to cut CETA and summer jobs by approximately half; if we wanted to eliminate new expenditure authority for programs like sewage treatment plants; if we wanted to eliminate all new public housing or publicly subsidized housing starts; if we wanted to reduce the amount that Congress contributes, on a sliding scale, to states for Medicaid by 6 percent, we could save $1.3 billion. We could cut Title XX social services by $350 million, in contrast to the $100 million by which it was raised in the budget resolution this time. We could eliminate half a million kids from Title I, the Elementary and Secondary Education Act, and we could cut every other state aid program in the budget by 7.5 percent. That would save, in all, about $9.5–10 billion.

The federally run domestic programs, which amount to about $62 billion, are often made up almost totally of personnel and services provided by personnel. The only way to save dollars there is to cut people; so we decided we would try to cut personnel costs by about 10 percent. But there is a catch: in order to cut personnel costs by 10 percent, we have to cut personnel by 20 percent, because of the separation costs when a federal employee is fired. We found we could save $2.5 billion there, which left us with $5 billion to go. We decided to eliminate all proposed new water projects and eight old ones, as well. I think it is understood how difficult that would be, given President Carter's experience the time he tried something similar.

At NASA we decided not to cut the space shuttle. Since we have already put $7 billion into the space shuttle, I assume we would not want to waste that money by dropping the program. Therefore, to take a proportionate share out of the space program, we would have to cut everything else but the shuttle program by approximately one-half.

We could also cut the Basic Opportunity Grant, which is the basic student aid program for every eligible kid who goes to college in this country. We could save some money by cutting those grants by $200 a head. That is what we had to do to get down to the amount needed to reduce those programs by their proportionate share, just as we cut every other program in the federal government.

In defense and international affairs, we cut foreign aid by approximately three-fourths, exempting most of the Middle East money but certainly not all of it. We decided that we would also have to eliminate all new procurement and reduce our defense force by approximately 210,000 people. That is the equivalent of five divisions.

By doing all this, we came to a total of $38 billion. Obviously, anyone doing this exercise could argue about individual programs, whether to cut here or there. We simply tried to cut every single federal program by the approximate share that it represents in the federal budget and cut the big-ticket items by even more in order to reach that mythical balanced budget as defined by the Congressional Budget Office.

Some will say that that is exaggerated, that we would not have to do it year after year once we have the budget in balance. But that is not so. Between 1974 and 1976, as Charles Schultze indicated, we would have had to cut a much larger percentage of federal expenditures than we would be required to cut today in order to achieve a balanced budget. And what does it all get us after we have finished? The CBO tells us that after going through all that, we would wind up with GNP down $60 billion, unemployment up about 1 percent, and inflation reduced by 0.1 percent.

I really would object to a mechanistic approach, such as a constitutionally mandated balanced budget amendment, to the problem of inflation because the approach does not match the problem. Even the present budget resolution system does not work very well precisely because it is so mechanistic.

As for the political implications, if I had my druthers and if I could control the Democratic party for two days, I would balance the budget. I would do it as a hard-nosed, tactical political maneuver, because it would bring a lot of people to an awareness that even after we balance the budget, we would still have inflation. That knowledge would probably benefit people more than anything else I could do. So, if I were not convinced that it would cause tremendous social and economic problems for the country, I would be tempted to engage in a little constructive irresponsibility and balance the budget this year. That would teach people something about the complex nature of the causes of inflation.

It Is Time
for a Serious Reform

James Dale Davidson

One of the problems with our discussion is that it goes in several directions. As is usually the case in life when people do not see eye to eye, we are really talking about different things. Congressman Obey has just given the perspective of someone who has to deal with a lot of difficult problems, with which I am glad I do not have to wrestle. I am not surprised that he does not see this issue quite the way I do.

In my view, the balanced budget drive goes right to the heart of a problem in our country: that there is no necessity that the political outcomes obtained in Washington relate very closely to the desires of the citizens. There is little doubt that if we had a referendum today, tomorrow, last year, in 1975, or five years from now without a balanced budget amendment, the public would disapprove the total of federal expenditures. We have a system that rewards organized special interests, and the tendency over time for these benefits to accumulate is irresistible. It is much more costly to an individual congressman to reduce an expenditure, even if it has proved to be absurd, than to go along with it and try to find the resources somewhere to finance it.

If it were true that the merits of the issues determined how expenditures were made, then there would be less support for many congressional programs after they had been in place for a few years. Beforehand, a person of good will might be deluded into thinking that something like the CETA program, the Head Start program, or what-have-you, would do the job. But we find that expenditures continue to rise without any particular connection to the observed benefits. No matter whether money is spent well or ill, it is always spent to the benefit of someone, and the people who get the money are, of course, very glad to have it. The problem is that the costs of this outrun the ability and the desire of the public to submit to taxes to pay for it, and this has led to chronic deficit spending. The reason for this is quite simple. We have heard from Dr. Schultze that human nature continues to be more or less the same, and I imagine that will be so until human beings evolve into a new species. Human nature is such that people respond to circumstances so as to maximize their rewards over cost.

Consider the case of congressmen. They vote for deficits because deficits enable them to shirk accountability for the costs of some of what they do. This is true in either of the two ways in which deficits are financed. If they are financed by inflation, owing to the monetization of the government debt, then some of the public wrath about this cost is diverted onto the labor unions and the local businesses, the gas stations and the supermarkets. If less than 100 percent of the public understand how inflation works, which is clearly the case, then there is an obvious benefit to politicians in incurring inflation as a way of financing the spending programs. If, on the other hand, the budget deficit is financed by real borrowing, then the money is obtained through the offering of an investment opportunity to individuals in the marketplace. That offering has to be priced to sell; otherwise, it will not. The people who obtain the bonds are not by any means suffering the cost. They are making an investment comparable to any other kind of investment. The people who will pay some of the costs for this borrowing are the future taxpayers who may come along some generations hence to redeem the debts. Since many of these are not of voting age at the present time and others are not even born, they clearly cannot be here to complain to Congressman Obey and his associates about what they do.

So deficit spending provides a clear benefit to the politicians. With deficit spending they can maximize their rewards over costs by deflecting some of these costs and disguising them in various ways. This I think has been recognized implicitly or explicitly by everyone. In fact, some of the objections we hear to a balanced budget amendment really come down to a recognition that this shirking of full accountability will continue no matter what we do. Dr. Schultze has told us we had better not attempt to make politicians accountable, because if we do, they will find another way of being unaccountable. They will mandate expenditures onto private persons directly; they will find other sneaky ways of imposing costs which the public at large does not wish to bear, in order to reward highly concentrated interests, what Bentham called "corrupt combinations of selfish interests." Dr. Schultze projects that with a balanced budget, regulatory costs would be increased and that taxes on wealth or other unmentionable devices might be found to shirk an honest accounting of the costs.

Now, it seems to me that this recognition indicates an implicit acceptance of our contention that politicians are bent upon spending as much as possible and disguising the costs as much as possible, to avoid being accountable to the public at large. If it is true that there will be an effort at displacement, so that high regulatory costs, let us say, would be sought on a dollar-per-dollar basis to equal the savings of social costs from curtailment of the deficit, then it still is not likely, in my estimation, that these regulatory costs could mount to the same degree. This is for a simple reason: when you impute a regulatory cost directly to some-body, the cost is explicit, which it is not in the case of a budget deficit. If, for instance, the private employer is told to hire or retain an employee over a certain period of time, all this does is increase the value of mechanization in the industry, or speed the flow of capital outside the country.

The cleverness of politicians in finding ways of imposing explicit costs upon people directly is matched by the vigor of the private sector in avoiding these costs. Therefore, it is hardly a disputable conclusion that if the costs are x from a budget deficit, and the displacement costs that the politicians would desire to impose would also be x, the total they would *succeed* in imposing would be x minus something.

Outraged reactions of the many spending constituencies to the idea of a balanced budget amendment are the best indication that the pro-posal would mean something. If an amendment would be meaningless, if all sorts of ways would be found to go around it, then the spending constituencies would be wasting their energy by bothering to oppose it.

In fact, they are howling like mad that a balanced budget rule would be the ruin of our country, and they are spending lots of money. An organization has been put together, including government employee groups and others who, quite rightly, predict that if a balanced budget amendment required Congress to own up explicitly to the costs of spend-ing, then the public would balk—and demand a lower level of expend-iture. So we see implicit evidence that the assumption behind a balanced budget amendment is not misleading, is not false. The opponents them-selves recognize that it is true, even though they usually do not say so explicitly.

Another point that I think does bear questioning was brought up by Professor Olson in the previous session. That is the suggestion that while it may be desirable to restrain the excessive costs that government imposes upon the economy, the outcomes that we face today essentially reflect the triumph of the Big Battalions of political power. We dare not challenge them by changing the Constitution because then we might discover that the Constitution really does not mean very much. The Big Battalions might just cast it aside and continue to reward themselves at the expense of the general public. We would then end up just as poor and perhaps more unhappy.

This is a very substantial argument. But I believe it is also true that the Constitution not only is a reflection of the raw power of various groups, but also helps determine that power. When rules change, out-comes change as well. Consider the example of Switzerland. It is an advanced industrial society, its GNP is very high, and it has no un-employment to speak of. It is true that Switzerland has a diversity of cultures and languages, and that the cantons are insular and jealous. They also have many of the same problems as all industrial societies, but far fewer of them because they have higher incomes and they have much less government. Taxes are far lower. I submit that one reason Swiss taxes are lower is that major tax increases have to be approved by the voters in referenda, not only by an overall majority, but by majorities in a majority of cantons. This, in effect, is a way of raising tremendously the cost of obtaining special benefits at the public expense. Because the cost of winning special benefits is much higher, more peo-ple, instead of diverting their energies into lobbying, go to work in the private sector and make clocks or some other thing.

We have clear evidence that the costs can be altered. The current lobbying legislation has altered the costs of certain ways of influencing Congress and state legislators. The campaign financing laws have altered the kinds of campaigns that can be run for president, which accounts to a certain extent for Dr. Schultze's present position, or at least his boss's present position. These points are beyond dispute. It is equally well within the range of human capacity to predict that if a balanced budget amendment of the right sort were passed, it would have precisely the kinds of effects which we are advocating and which I think the majority of the American people favor.

Let me speak for a moment to some of the other questions that have been raised. We talk here as if the amendment has already been written, proposed, and enacted, and yet we do not really know what type of amendment thoughtful people would devise. That is one reason I favor a constitutional convention. I believe that the delegates to a convention, given that they have fewer day-to-day interests to maintain, might take a longer view. One of the people who I hope might be elected to a constitutional convention, who I know will never be a senator from Pennsylvania, is Professor Allan Meltzer, the author of a very simple draft amendment. It is quite succinct, and it does come to grips with the problem Anthony Downs raised in the last session, when he said that a balanced budget amendment would not affect in-flation.

We all know that inflation is not caused directly by budget deficits, but rather by the increase of the money supply which is used to accom-modate these deficits. In today's society, it is a superfluous truth to say that the deficits do not cause inflation. However, it is true also that the government could, without deficits, create as much inflation as it pleased by simply monetizing private debt, or by literally printing money. So an object of any good amendment would be to place a cost upon the government for increasing inflation. Professor Meltzer's proposal is worded:

> Total government outlays in any fiscal year shall not exceed the spending limit. The spending limit is equal to the average of total budget receipts in the three most recent fiscal years.

In other words, if you have revenues in three fiscal years of eight dollars, ten dollars, and twelve dollars, the spending limit in the next fiscal year would be ten dollars. Since the limit is established in nominal terms, the effect of this amendment in the event of a genuine downturn would not be countercyclical. It would enable the government to spend up to the spending limit even if revenues fell below previous levels.

On the other hand, if the inflation rate were high, the effective size of the surplus would be increased. The government would suffer a penalty for incurring inflation, which, as we all know, is the opposite of the current situation. As Russell Long has demonstrated to his colleagues who could not understand it, inflation has the effect of ratcheting people up into higher tax brackets. So Congress can go through the show of reducing taxes while actually increasing real tax rates. Over the last decade, income has risen by 10 percent but tax rates have increased by 16.5 percent, hardly a happy result. We can come to grips with this by altering the costs and rewards to congressmen of creating inflation. This amendment would give politicians a much higher incentive to reduce taxes than to enact new programs. If they inflated like wild to push people up into higher tax brackets, they would not be able to spend the money anyway. They would probably return it in the form of tax reductions.

Another problem addressed by the Meltzer proposal is that of wild and woolly accounting tricks which could be introduced to get around a constraint. Professor Meltzer's plan states: "Total government outlays include all budget and off-budget expenditures plus the present value of commitments for future outlays." This one very simple sentence comes to grips with the problem of off-budget outlays, interest subsidies, loan guarantees, and so forth.

The third point of the Meltzer plan does in one paragraph everything that the tax limitation plan does in several pages. It states: "The rate of growth of total budget receipts shall not exceed the rate of growth of an appropriate index of the economy in the most recently completed calendar year." Instead of writing GNP into the Constitution, we allow Congress to define the index: "The index shall be chosen by the Congress and may be changed by two-thirds vote of each house." This is a forward-looking proposition. In the event that Congress wishes

138

to change the definitions, we require that they do so by a super majority so as not to evade the intent of the limit.

Further, we have a solution to the objection that it would be unwise in certain circumstances to have a balanced budget—a valid point. A very simple way around the difficulty is an emergency clause: "In the event that an emergency is declared by the president, the Congress may, by two-thirds vote of each house, authorize outlays for that fiscal year in excess of the spending limit." Finally, Meltzer suggests that Congress enact all necessary legislation to implement the amendment, which resolves the question of who is to have jurisdiction in the event that Congress fails to do its job.

Many, if not most, of the objections to an amendment can be handled simply by judicious wording. Therefore, while a balanced budget is not a panacea, it would do what the people basically want, which is to come to grips with the excessive growth of government spending. It would prohibit politicians from following their tendency to impose long-term costs on the economy in exchange for short-term benefits to themselves. To some extent, it would also weaken the coalitions of powerful, selfish interest groups. If the total pie is more or less fixed, groups would tend to break out of log-rolling coalitions and start looking instead for ways to cut money out of one another's budget. That would become a more likely source of additional revenues than a deficit passed on to the general public.

I think that the 80 percent or so of the public of the United States who favor a constitutional amendment to balance the budget have correctly perceived the problem. The solution we offer would do much of what they want. It is not a perfect reform, but nothing in human conduct ever is. The best course of action, it seems to me, is to move forward with the alternatives we have. If in future times it proves that regulation or some other deflected cost becomes too onerous, then let the future find an appropriate response. They would need, as we need now, something that takes into account the rewards and costs to the individual politicians, something that applies in the public sector the same observations that have been so important in helping us to understand the rest of life. That is, we should look at outcomes not in terms of what is desirable on a moral basis, but rather in terms of a behavioral analysis of individual action.

The Feasibility of an Amendment: Some Legal and Political Considerations

Ralph K. Winter

With a problem like this, one has to start at the beginning and ask what the criteria are for deciding when to amend the Constitution. Naturally, we would not want to adopt an amendment for every whimsical and transitory movement that comes along. We either have to have the abiding conviction that there exists an evil so great that it is worth the sacrifice of removing the issue from the normal democratic political process or have to believe that the normal democratic political process is in some sense defective in handling a particular issue.

I lean toward the conclusion that some kind of balanced budget amendment may satisfy the first criterion and does satisfy the second, but I am not persuaded that an amendment is feasible.

The first criterion may be satisfied in that the ever-increasing expenditures by government could lead to an ever-contracting private sector, with all the implications that has not only for the economy but for our political democracy. If significant inflation is, in fact, a chronic political compromise between strident public demands for greater expenditures and equally strident protests against higher taxation, that situation may be such a great evil that we need an amendment. Printing money may be, after all, less politically visible than a direct reduction in government expenditures or a direct increase in taxes. It reduces the value of expenditures, and it may elevate people through tax brackets or otherwise increase the amount of taxes they actually pay. And, as Mr. Davidson has indicated, government-caused inflation is also dandy in the sense that it can be blamed on other groups.

All of us, both political parties and all ideological groups, share the blame for this. All presidents do it. All presidents blame inflation on the private sector: the unions, corporations, whatever; whatever companies Pat Caddell happens to say are unpopular that week are almost invariably targeted as causes of inflation.

If the experience of New York City, where ever-increasing taxes destroyed the private sector, is the harbinger of what we are going to face, then an amendment would be justifiable. As I understand the figures, Mayor John Lindsay's jobs program created 150,000 new public

140

jobs in New York City, while destroying half a million private sector jobs. As a deputy mayor once confirmed, New York City would not have any problems if it could print its own money. I can testify from personal experience that he had an inadequate legal education.

The second criterion may be met in that the welfare state appears to spread its benefits across the board to all segments of society, not just to the genuinely needy. The welfare state simply does not correspond to the rhetoric that is deployed to justify it. It is more likely that the welfare state spreads its benefits according to political power. The increase in what are called social welfare expenditures has been so vast in the last two decades, that if we were worried about the genuinely needy, we could have given that money to the 25 million poorest people in the country, and a poor family of four would then have had an income above the median. It is not lack of money, therefore; it is just that it is spread across so many groups.

The examples that have been mentioned are the veterans' programs, the farm programs, and aid to education. I have some experience in local education, and I know that increasing expenditures in local education is not helping kids; it is paying teachers. It is just increasing the salaries of those particular government employees. The school lunch program fights poverty at the fanciest private schools, and many programs that really do seem designed to help the poor seem also to help middle-class professionals.

The reason for this spreading around is that very few people perceive that the benefits they receive from government are really a significant cause of higher taxes, inflation, or even government size, or, conversely, that if the programs that benefit them were eliminated, then there would in fact be smaller government and less taxation and less inflation. Most people just do not see any connection, and they are right because their share of the pot is so small.

What a majority in the country may instinctively feel, however, is that eliminating the programs that help them along with the vast number of other programs would lead to a net benefit—that they would be made better off by an across-the-board cut.

The trouble is that candidate-versus-candidate politics does not offer you that option. Every group fears that its act of self-abnegation may be in vain, that they will wind up losing their programs but there will be no across-the-board cut. So everybody says, "You go ahead and eliminate your demands, and then I'll come along and eliminate mine." The political process really does not offer voters a candidate who can credibly promise across-the-board cuts.

In this competition every group, no matter what its ideological orientation, feels it has to grab its share or some other group will get there first. This leads to an array of claims that cannot be satisfied fiscally but are impossible to deny politically.

We have political campaigns in which everyone is anti-Washington, but the right promises are made to particular groups. The most aggravated situation of all is New York City. What was the issue in the last democratic mayoral primary? The fiscal problems of New York City? No, the death penalty. The mayor has no authority over the death penalty, but the candidates stumped on the issue up and down the city.

The problem is not that Congress is full of people who do not know what they are doing. They are doing exactly what they are being asked to do, because nobody will sacrifice their benefits without assurance from others that they will sacrifice theirs. This is relevant to a constitutional amendment because an amendment limiting the fiscal authority of government does allow an all-together approach, does provide assurance that across-the-board cuts or limitations will take place. It is on this basis that one can justify advocating an amendment.

On the other hand, a convention is probably the last thing we really want. We are not talking about a major revision of the Constitution; we are talking about specific amendments directed to a specific problem. These amendments face very significant drafting problems that really ought to be studied in Congress with due deliberation.

Senator Griffin suggested that people might be against a constitutional convention because it would be used by some unknown people to make themselves better known. I worry about that. I think it would be a circus. We should remember that the Convention of 1787 took place before Common Cause, and it was held in private, to the extent that major documentary evidence of intent was not available for a generation.

If we had a constitutional convention today, it would be clouded with doubt about its constitutionality. The nation's eyes would be focused on that question and on all the crazy proposals that would come up. It seems to me exactly the wrong way to go about it.

My concern about feasibility could be wrong. I think one can probably get a limit on spending and a relatively satisfactory formula for doing it. If I have identified the defect correctly, there ought to be a limit on spending. It is not taxation or an unbalanced budget; it is government spending and the pressure for it that we ought to counteract. I am satisfied there are ways to do this.

However, I see three great problems. The first is enforceability, a problem that the amendment itself must take care of, at least in part. We should not have a situation in which, as I understand Mr. Davidson's amendment, no one can sue if Congress does nothing. The requirements for standing to sue are, I urge you to understand, in the Constitution. They are not in statutes; they are in the Constitution. If a constitutional amendment is to be enforceable, that amendment must create the standing. Congress cannot do it.

In addition, we need somebody to be sued. I hope it is not being overtechnical to suggest that we need a defendant in most lawsuits, and that defendant has to have legal authority over the matters the suit concerns. That is, the defendant must be able to limit spending. I am not prepared to leave matters like that to some future action by Congress. In addition, we should not have everybody in the country as a potential plaintiff. We cannot have several million lawsuits filed in the district courts around the country with different attorneys trying to prosecute conflicting claims about the budget. Also, as Dr. Schultze says, we have to limit the issues that go to the courts. We have to have a plaintiff, a defendant, and an issue well enough defined that the courts can handle it. Then there can be a trial and people can introduce evidence and a court can reach a judgment.

The alternative is to have an amendment like the provision in the Constitution saying that members of Congress cannot have commissions in the Armed Forces. The Supreme Court of the United States has held that this is essentially unenforceable because there is nobody injured by it who can bring suit. We have to be careful when we are drafting an amendment such as this that we do not leave it unenforceable, as some of the current provisions in the Constitution actually are.

Another problem is national defense versus contractual claims. The government has made promises, through a variety of programs like social security, that we all know are fraudulent. What would the FTC do to a company that said, "You pay me $100 per month and when you get old, I'll pay you what I feel like." Still, other citizens regard these programs as promises of our government, and that has to be understood when you draft this amendment.

The final problem is the possibility of government-mandated private spending, which Mr. Davidson talked about. When OSHA forces companies to spend money on certain things, it is functionally equivalent to the government's spending the money itself. We could have national health insurance without really having any increase in the budgetary expenditures of the federal government. Now, I do not know how to define that kind of spending; I do not think we can. If we tried to prohibit it, we would probably cripple the government. Maybe Mr. Davidson is right that the fear is unjustified. But if we limit only explicit spending, we force the political pressures to spend into other channels; and these other channels may be even more destructive and inefficient than explicit government spending. I may be wrong about this, but I fear that the cost will be borne by a narrow group that is not particularly popular.

It is true, as Mr. Davidson said, that there are sanctions. Capital would be driven out of the country, and that would be very damaging. On the other hand, our experience has certainly not been that the government is afraid of driving capital out of the country.

Discussion

SENATOR GRIFFIN: Let me ask Mr. Davidson a question that I think is on the minds of a lot of people. We read in the papers about the number of states that have adopted resolutions calling for a constitutional convention. What is the status of your drive to get thirty-four states? Where are you? Do you think you are going to get thirty-four states? When? And, assuming that you are optimistic and will say that you expect to reach that magic number, perhaps we could then get some response from Senator Lugar and from Congressman Obey regarding what Congress will do if and when thirty-four states actually file petitions.

MR. DAVIDSON: We have a prospect of getting the thirty-four states within a year's time. We have already got thirty states in less time than has ever been done before in the history of the country. When thirty-one states called for a convention back at the turn of the century, it had taken approximately nine years to reach that number. That was a call for a convention on the direct election of senators.

We now have twenty states from which to pick four. Legislative elections are coming up in many of these states, which may put us in an easier position than before because we can target our efforts on a smaller base. And, of course, we have other considerations to bear in mind. We have a gentleman in California who may, indeed, decide to run for president. If he does so, I think he will be much less gentle in terms of his fight for the call for the convention in that state than he was in the current session, because many of the legislators who are up for reelection in California could face primary opposition, which I suspect is the last thing they would want. Therefore, I hope that some of the legislators who were inclined to vote against the balanced budget amendment in California will turn around. The prospect is good that we will eventually succeed in California. Then, a couple of other states in the Midwest and in the East might act on this; Kentucky is a good prospect, I think.

We may have the thirty-four states by February or March 1980. If

145

Congress fails to act, then we will have an opportunity to see who else can do the job. I do not share Professor Winter's fear of a constitutional convention. I think that a convention, if it were convened, would draw upon good people, people who would not be candidates for Congress or probably would not want to be, with all respect to Congressman Obey. They probably would not want to stay in Washington long enough to qualify for a pension. Indeed, we hope the constitutional convention could complete its activities in less than ten years.

SENATOR GRIFFIN: Congressman Obey, if the reports arrive in March 1980 that thirty-four states have adopted resolutions calling for a constitutional convention, what will the House and Senate do?

CONGRESSMAN OBEY: I am really not in a position to say, because that issue would be dealt with in the Judiciary Committee, as you know. I am neither a lawyer nor a member of the Judiciary Committee, and I am proud of one of those facts. My assumption is that they will first make an assessment of whether they really received thirty-four. While I am in no position to evaluate this, I hear from people on that committee that there is no great fear of really getting thirty-four because of the great divergence in the nature of the resolutions sent to Congress.

SENATOR LUGAR: I would add simply that, given the composition of the Judiciary Committees of the House and Senate, both would probably conclude that thirty-four states are not there. They would throw out this petition and that petition, engage in quite a bit of sparring, and try to delay things as much as possible.

SENATOR GRIFFIN: At least until after the 1980 elections?

SENATOR LUGAR: That is a close calculation that somebody like Senator Robert Byrd, the majority leader, will attempt to make at that point. Would it be preferable for candidates of his party to go to the country having just voted for a constitutional amendment? Or have the polls shifted, and could the party's candidates risk appearing dilatory? I would guess that Senator Byrd will probably attempt to confuse the issue by bringing forward a resolution a good bit stiffer than anything that we've seen before. In other words, he might propose legislation, as opposed to a constitutional amendment, to balance the budget. This would give all Democrats something to vote for, as they leave to campaign, that showed voters how intensely they felt about this. That way, they could campaign on a balanced budget platform again, as I recall they did in 1978, and, having staved off electoral defeat in 1980, come back and stall some more.

I think that the votes are not there now. A two-thirds majority of both houses is needed to propose a constitutional amendment. On the other hand, it is not yet clear what the sentiments will be in 1980 and what sort of an issue this might turn out to be.

SENATOR GRIFFIN: Are you assuming that they would not recognize that there are thirty-four resolutions?

SENATOR LUGAR: That would be the first tack. Then, having not recognized it, Senator Byrd would have to decide whether to proceed with some action anyway while Congress still had the ball in its court.

PROFESSOR GROVER REES, University of Texas Law School: The argument about cluttering up the Constitution is a legitimate concern. I am worried about it, as I think most people are, but it seems to me it is used rather selectively. It was first used by Senator Bayh and Congressman Edwards against abortion amendments, antibusing amendments, balanced budget amendments, spending limitation amendments, school prayer amendments. They felt all these things were passing fancies that we might think differently about next year, and therefore we do not want to clutter up the Constitution with them. However, the very same people have produced ERA and the amendment to give Washington, D.C., two senators. I suggest that that is analogous to giving the Richard Viguerie Company two senators, in terms of the results it would produce. They are also pushing to abolish the electoral college. I do not think there is any great widespread support for at least some of these ideas around the country, and yet they have not been worried about cluttering up the Constitution when it comes to their proposals. Amendments that have been passed in the last few years—the eighteen-year-old vote, which should have been left up to the state legislatures; moving Inauguration Day; abolishing state poll taxes, D.C. voting—are also things that we did not worry about cluttering up the Constitution with when we passed them.

Senator Kennedy has compounded the deception, I think, by saying that the constitutional convention process is the darker side of the amending process, to wit: the side not currently controlled by Senator Kennedy. And we must not think that by having a very selective concern against cluttering up the Constitution, we are not cheapening that argument. We are reducing its availability for a time when we might really need it, when there might be some truly dangerous or frivolous amendment, as I do not think abortion or balanced budgets or any of these

147

things is. Don't you think, Congressman Obey, that you are driving the people who feel frustrated at their inability to get things through Congress to this darker side of the amending process?

CONGRESSMAN OBEY: I should start by thanking you for your endorsement of the leadership of the Democratic party across the board. I do not feel any special responsibility to defend the action or the statement of any other member of Congress; I will just take my own position here. I think there is a distinct difference between what we are talking about in this case and things like the D.C. voting rights amendment and the eighteen-year-old voting amendment. Basically, when you are dealing with the question of government spending, you are concerned about the level of taxation. The other amendments are not concerned with whether taxes are too high or too low. They are different in nature from placing in the Constitution an economic philosophy. It is legitimate for Congress to take an interest in whether people under twenty-one years of age or people who are citizens of Washington, D.C., can exercise the franchise. I do not regard it as a trivial matter to state, in a constitutional way, whether a female has the same inherent rights as a male. I do not regard these things as on the same level with questions of who is right and who is wrong about an approach to spending policy; they are quite different matters.

LINCOLN C. OLIPHANT, Office of Senator Jake Garn: Professor Winter, suppose that in the spring of 1980 we have thirty-four identical calls for a convention, but Congress refuses to call one, as Senator Lugar, I think quite rightly, suspects. What, if anything, is the remedy, or is this one of those conventional provisions that has no remedy? If the National Taxpayers Union hired you, what would be your advice?

PROFESSOR WINTER: We would talk about the fee first; advice would follow.

My advice to them may be different from what I think ought to happen. I feel very strongly that the failure of Congress to call a convention would be a political question. The courts ought not get involved; the remedy is to vote against those senators and congressmen who fail to call the convention.

It is not the courts' business to hand down a mandatory injunction that a constitutional convention be called.

SENATOR GRIFFIN: Then is the deliberate use of the word *shall* in Article V meaningless? They could have said *may*.

148

PROFESSOR WINTER: The language may seem mandatory, but that does not necessarily mean that it is judicially enforceable. The style of the Warren Court was to find all kinds of mandatory things in the Constitution, but this seems to me to be one of those constitutional issues that is best left ultimately to the people.

MR. DAVIDSON: It sounds like his advice is not the type we would like to hire.

DAVID KEATING, National Taxpayers Union: Do you think the Supreme Court could issue some sort of declaratory judgment instead of just refusing to rule?

PROFESSOR WINTER: There may be no clear remedy to be given. You have to decide how the convention will be constituted and all sorts of other issues. I do not want the Supreme Court of the United States deciding it. The Supreme Court is already deciding all kinds of things it should not be deciding. Part of our current problems result from the Court's reading the Constitution as an affirmative grant of power to it to make up rules even without anything in the Constitution to back them up. This is the kind of question on which the Constitution does not provide sufficiently specific standards for judicial action.

MR. DAVIDSON: The explicit language in Article V says that Congress shall call a constitutional convention upon application of two-thirds of the state legislatures. If we grant that thirty-four states have done so, that would seem to me as clear as anything could be.

PROFESSOR REES: If you need a legal opinion in your favor on this justiciability issue, it is very much an open question, think of *Powell* v. *McCormack*. The Court told the House that they could not expel Adam Clayton Powell under the guise of excluding him (which I think was quite proper for the Court to do). The Court told the state legislature in Tennessee in *Baker* v. *Carr* to take affirmative action and reconstruct itself, as I also think was quite proper. If the Court can do these things, then it can certainly enjoin Congress to pass something that it says in the Constitution Congress shall pass. The first duty of the Court is to say what the law is, and that is what the law is. The origin of the political questions doctrine, back in Andrew Jackson's time, was based on the Court's fear that Congress would not listen.

PROFESSOR WINTER: But consider the questions the Court would have to answer if it asserted jurisdiction. How many representatives to the

149

convention will each state have? How many votes will each state have? Who will convene it?

PROFESSOR REES: I admit there would be problems in working that out, but the Court could order them to . . .

PROFESSOR WINTER: Order them to what?

PROFESSOR REES: To convene the same kind of convention . . .

PROFESSOR WINTER: Order the Senate of the United States to pass a resolution of some kind?

PROFESSOR REES: Yes, they could, just as they issued a declaratory judgment saying that Adam Clayton Powell was entitled to his seat.

PROFESSOR WINTER: You are a child of the Warren Court, my boy.

PROFESSOR REES: Those are fighting words.

SENATOR LUGAR: As a practical matter, the question still would finally be resolved in elections of members of the Senate and House. Without knowing how the Court would go about this, I think that even if the Court accepted this case, it would find good reason not to reach a decision very rapidly, despite all the demands of the parties. So we would be back once again to the Judiciary Committees of the House and the Senate who now see a ticking bomb over at the Supreme Court going off at some unspecified time in the future.

What this finally comes down to is a presumption on my part, and on the part of many, that a large majority of the people of the country want spending limited and they want the budget balanced in one form or another. If that is incorrect, then the budget balancing is not going to happen, either through the Constitution or in practice. If it is correct, the net effect of trying to give a runaround to thirty-four or more state legislatures, and to what appears to be the will of the people, will be for many senators and members of the House to court defeat. It may not happen all in the same election, but there is already a good bit of genuflecting in the direction of budget balancing, as we saw in the 1978 election, and it will be even more pronounced in 1980. Those who do not quite pick it up that fast may not be with us, and, essentially, we will move toward a political solution. I think this is the proper way to do it.

Otherwise, you get into the type of thing that we are facing on an entirely different issue with Barry Goldwater's suit on the Taiwan Treaty termination. The question is whether the president can terminate this treaty by himself, or whether he needs two-thirds of the Senate as well. This is the kind of suit the Court is reluctant to get into. It is like the Nixon papers; there is incentive to drag it on and on forever to avoid a collision between the branches of government. I think that a political solution will be found.

PETER FURTH, Louis Furth, Inc.: Senator Lugar, I am getting the impression that perhaps you would rather not see a constitutional amendment, but that you are trying to move the political process and the political forces in certain directions and using this as your method. Am I correct?

SENATOR LUGAR: No, I think the amendment would be a good thing, and I do not have any ambivalence in that regard. I do believe the whole discussion of the amendment has led political forces in a direction that I find more compatible with my own views, and I think that will continue to be the case. But this is not a "dog in the manger" argument.

I believe that the forces for spending and restraint are unequal. A balancing of the sides, structurally, is required, and an amendment offers enough presumption for restraint to bring it into balance with spending. That is why I believe it has a place in the Constitution.

MR. FURTH: Would you be satisfied to see the process lead to the passage and enforcement of the sort of bill that you thought Senator Byrd might propose?

SENATOR LUGAR: No, because I think it would have about the same effect as the resolution we pass each year raising the national debt ceiling. It is done twice a year and as often as necessary, and always on the basis that if we did not do it, we could not pay the armed forces or social security recipients the following third of the month.

What we are looking at here is a procedure. A budget balancing amendment is not going to happen instantly. It will require some debate in Congress and, beyond that, two or three years, perhaps, for three-fourths of the states to ratify it. The idea takes some getting used to. Gradually, the country will become used to the presumption of balance, and I think it is important that there be an adjustment period.

CHRISTOPHER J. WARNER, Office of Senator William Roth: One of the arguments for the convention is that Congress will not act. That is the political argument. Another argument that I think people are starting

151

to bring up is that Congress cannot act with discipline in the fiscal process. We are seeing with the convention drive a mood among a lot of citizens for quick fixes that do not involve going to Congress, that involve somehow doing it through some other process. You see that with Proposition 13; you see it with some of the tax limitation proposals. It seems that Congress now is becoming a case-working body; people are going to Congress for "gimme" types of things, whereas they are going for the quick fixes, the balanced budget amendment, the convention, or some sort of citizens' movement, in order to make policy. Would the congressional members of the panel comment on that?

CONGRESSMAN OBEY: Everybody who has spoken about the difficulty of forcing Congress to make choices is absolutely correct. For instance, I have in my storeroom bootleg computer printouts from the National Cancer Institute that lay out virtually every contract that is let out there. Richard Nixon and Edward Kennedy stumbled all over themselves ten years ago to show who is more against cancer. So we passed the National Cancer Act and shoveled money into it, but we did not provide the personnel to oversee the contracts, and we have, in my judgment, wasted at least a third of the money we spent under the aegis of the National Cancer Act in the last ten years.

Now, that is true in many, many areas, but the problem I have with this constitutional amendment approach is that people are looking for, to quote, a "quick fix." What separates me from Mr. Davidson and Senator Lugar is that they think they know what the answer is, and I do not. I do suspect that it is not in the direction of trying to duplicate what we do in the budget process.

What we do in the budget process (this was the "answer" just a few years ago) is spend three and a half weeks on the House floor sending a resolution to ourselves. That is exactly what we did this year. We tell ourselves and the world what we are going to do; then after we tell ourselves what we are going to do, we proceed to do it; and then after we do it, we pass another resolution telling ourselves what we did. The problem is that in the same amount of time that it took us to pass the budget resolution, we could take every appropriation bill and let the appropriation subcommittees report it to the House; we could take every entitlement bill and report that to the House; we could take whatever tax bill is going to be considered and report it to the House; and then refer it all to the Budget Committee. Then we would let the Budget Committee review the priorities and the amounts being suggested in that package, as well as the taxation phiiosophy, and bring it to the floor with a substitute amendment in order from the committee, if they want. This is to say we could spend our time dealing with the real legislation rather than simply with a budget, which is a mechanistic way of setting limits, that really does not do much at all.

My concern with this movement is that I think it dissipates a lot of energy that can be used in a direct way to accomplish the changes we need within the Congress in order to get intelligent review of program value. I think the way you do that is to start with the elimination of the one-year authorization process, which most committee chairmen mistakenly think gives them a short leash over government agencies.

Our problem, in my judgment, is that program oversight on the part of authorization committees is largely nonexistent. The only time you have oversight, really, with the exception of Government Operations or the Appropriations Committees which have tried to move into the breach, is when that same program is up for reauthorization. People usually use those hearings to justify their position for or against the reauthorization of the program, rather than being able to look at the performance of any program in a dispassionate way.

I agree with Senator Lugar that in the end this will probably be resolved through the political process. I believe that is what should happen, and I think that, for good or ill, Congress is all we have. I believe that we should spend our time trying to make that place truly function, by changing that authorization cycle so that you free up members' time to deal with real problems, if you can, for instance, limit the tendency of members of Congress to get on every committee in sight. We all have great egos and we all know that our ideas on a subject are as good or better than anybody else's, so we want to participate in the discussion of all the issues because they interest all of us, and, as a result, we know very little about any of it; we are not able to specialize in such a way that we can really deal with those problems effectively.

MR. DAVIDSON: There is a basic difference of opinion here as to what the logic of choice is and how it would affect Congress in the event that an amendment were passed. I point to something that occurred in the wake of Proposition 13. When the shock hit the various spending constituencies in California that Proposition 13 had not only passed but passed by a sizable majority, many of them began to point the finger at one another for being wastrels. All of a sudden, groups that had been engaged in the past in logrolling coalitions said, "Don't close down the library; the fire trucks are full of chrome, they don't have to be full of chrome. Let's make them just plain, paint them, you know, and don't cut back the school." The constituencies that previously had been united in favor of additional spending suddenly began to see the waste in one another's expenditures. I think that the logic is the same in terms of the balanced budget amendment.

153

Now to the specific command regarding Congress as a case-finding body that cannot act with fiscal discipline. The time Congress spends now debating the budget resolutions is well spent, and I should hate to deprive them of it. There is an old saying that no man's life or property is safe when the legislature is in session. If we could keep them debating the budget around the clock, all the time, it would be better than the alternatives. But if Professor Meltzer's plan were in effect, there would be no question what the spending limit would be. It would be known in advance from a simple arithmetical computation. Then the politicians would really have a chance to perform an oversight function, because that would be the only way they could free up additional funds with which to ply the special constituencies most prominent in their own districts.

But I would like to add something else to throw light on the question whether Congress is capable of making fiscal policy. This is an important question—it gets at the reason why people are now thinking of constitutional conventions or referenda, initiatives, and so on to obtain a political result which they desire but which seems otherwise unobtainable. The answer is that the cumulative effect of all the logrolling and back-scratching is such that many people now recognize that they lose more than they gain from this great shuffle and divide. They recognize that this outcome is a consequence of the institution of Congress itself.

This may help solve one of the mysteries in political theory, which is why congressmen continue to be reelected even though large majorities in every poll rate congressmen less efficacious as a group than garbagemen. What appears to be a paradox arises from the fact that the people, as a whole, think that the institution of Congress itself is at fault, not their particular congressman who they know is a great fellow. And so we return to the same point we have been trying to make all along: that we need to change the decision rules so that we come up with an outcome akin to what the public wants. If democracy has any moral force at all, it rests with that.

PATTY PRADO, Bank of America, San Francisco: Mr. Davidson, I realize that you favor the balanced budget amendment. Does this mean that you oppose alternative proposals, such as a constitutional limitation on spending? And if so, why?

MR. DAVIDSON: I do not think we have the final answer. I must have given Congressman Obey the wrong impression, because I believe, basically, that there is no panacea to this problem. It has been a long struggle and one that I think is best put in historical perspective as one of many alterations we have had to make in our system. We had, in the beginning, indirect election of senators; the framers did not really envision a political party system or they probably would not have given us the Electoral College. Certainly, there are many types of solutions which could be made, and many of them probably will be needed.

I do not oppose a tax limitation or a spending limitation. I do think that Professor Meltzer's proposal is quite good in that it combines the salient features of both proposals. But, again, it is a question of trying to do the best we can within the limitations of our circumstances.